Like Trees Walking

Like Trees Walking

In the Second Half of Life

Jane Sigloh

COWLEY PUBLICATIONS

Lanham, Chicago, New York, Toronto, and Plymouth, UK

Published by Cowley Publications
An imprint of Rowman & Littlefield Publishers, Inc.
A wholly owned subsidiary of The Rowman & Littlefield Publishing
Group, Inc.
4501 Forbes Boulevard, Suite 200
Lanham, MD 20706

Estover Road
Plymouth PL6 7PY
United Kingdom

Distributed by National Book Network

Library of Congress Cataloging-in-Publication Data

Sigloh, Jane, 1934–
    Like trees walking : in the second half of life / Jane Sigloh.
        p. cm.
    Includes bibliographical references.
    ISBN-13: 978-1-56101-290-9 (pbk. : alk. paper)
    ISBN-10: 1-56101-290-4 (pbk. : alk. paper)
        1. Older Christians—Religious life. 2. Aging—Religious aspects—
Christianity. I. Title.
BV4580.S54 2007
242'.65—dc22   2007005668

Printed in the United States of America.

⊚™ The paper used in this publication meets the minimum
requirements of American National Standard for Information
Sciences—Permanence of Paper for Printed Library Materials,
ANSI/NISO Z39.48-1992.

This book is dedicated with deep love and gratitude to my husband, Denny, who continues to believe that I am called to the ministry of the Word even though I am full of years.

ᴥ Contents

Looking Back

Under the Shadows

The Last Few Miles

Heading Home

Crossing the Jordan

❧ Foreword

YEARS ago I made my last visit to my grandmother. She had been confined to bed for several weeks, and everyone who knew anything realized that she was dying, though no one wanted to admit that aloud. She lay small and distant under white sheets, and the movements of her body were so slight they were like stillness itself. I remember that she sipped some coffee when it was offered, and she held her false teeth in one lightly cupped hand as if she might need them if she got miraculously hungry. My wife and I had brought our four young children with us, and I was not prepared for the sudden tears I was blinking back or for my helplessness in trying to deny the reality of my grandmother's impending death or at least to mask my response to it.

Except for my tears I literally had no words or actions—nothing at all—to offer.

Then my grandmother opened her eyes and looked at us and said the last words I was to hear her speak: "We just grow old," she said, and shut her eyes as if that was that. She died a few days later.

Over the years I have thought a lot about those four bald words and the mystery that unfolds out of them.

I kept thinking about them recently as I was reading Jane Sigloh's meditations on aging. For me these reflections offer a series of lights angling into and illuminating my grandmother's words, the truth that we all—if we are lucky—grow old.

Of course, we don't like to think about it, aging. Our natural inclination to ignore it is very strong and made even stronger by the blandishments of popular culture which convince us that proper diet and exercise, appropriate drugs (both prescription and across-the-counter), clever financial strategies, and really *really* positive thinking will give us, if not immortality, at least the ability to go on indefinitely.

Jane Sigloh will have none of that. It is important, she says—no, it is crucial—to reflect on aging and to make it personal, *our* aging, not just generic growing old. And paradoxically she pushes us to self-reflection by reflecting on her own aging in ways that are comic, bemusing, strange, assured and self-doubting, searching and finding: just like life itself.

How does she pull it off?

By starting with a description of a wren's nest, a memory of her grandfather taking her on his daily constitutional, an account of finding a note from her grandchild's kindergarten teacher, an image of milk delivered to the back door in bottles with cream on top, a depiction of an elderly Sunday School teacher whose power was the power of story, or a striking observation: "Young people think they invented sex."

And from that starting point allowing her thoughts to meander—or *seem* to meander (she knows where she is going and conveys that fact to the reader and creates the trust which any guide needs in order to assure her pilgrim that they are together headed somewhere true). Each reflection is in fact a journey, self-contained and complete, but each is also part of a longer journey into a deepened awareness of the pleasures, pains, absurdities, and oddities of old age.

Jane Sigloh is neither sentimental nor inattentive. She recognizes age as a "relentless series of losses," and she is exact in her depiction of the awful possibility that retirement, for most of us—in anticipation—the one bright spot in our imagined old age, can in reality debilitate us with boredom, anxiety, and depression. She recognizes that old age for most—for *all* if it goes on long enough—is a giving up of power. She stares balefully at the youthful Solomon singing the pleasures of the flesh because she remembers that at the end he was declaring that "all are from dust and all turn to dust again."

But neither is she cynical or despairing. She mines a deep vein of stories, both her own and those she has read. She asks us to re-see Adam and Eve, Moses, Samuel, Solomon, Saul, David, and—of course above all—Abraham and Sarah, those quintessential nonagenarians caught up by God into miracles so extravagant that the two couldn't resist laughing themselves into their son's very name. She has a suspicion of nostalgia, and she recognizes that dwelling in it can lead to nattering verbal rambling, but she knows too that while the good old days were not so good that you'd want to go back and live in them, true deep longing for the stories which shaped our lives can also inform our futures, like memories of the Red Sea parting and an empty tomb.

And she is always aware that even as we age (and sometimes because we do) life is literally grace-full, offering holy work which may be no more than making biscuits and shelling peas with a grandchild, learning to love fishing because it is the favorite activity of the beloved companion we are joyous to have still with us, or taking a morning walk to the mailbox at the end of the driveway, where we shouldn't be surprised to encounter Jesus. ("That would be nice," she suggests!)

The "lessons"—for those who want and need them—are never tacked on. They are always earned as part of the journey which each reflection invites us to take. The stereotypical nursing home which she names "Sunshine Haven" can slowly and reluctantly reveal the possibility of community and purpose. Falling backwards and landing turtle-like on a hike ultimately reveals, with a little help from St. Paul's understanding of "charity," that sometimes it is more truly blessed to receive than to give. This sort of imagining, and imaginativeness, allows Jane Sigloh to probe her own certain death and the eternity to which her journey is leading. And that probing, paradoxically, invites us into the pleasure of imagining our own dying and rising.

These witty, wise, often profound meditations are a gift, a vade mecum for those of us who cluster just around seventy or beyond. But they are also a gift to those who feel even in their youth the coming on of age, who observe the aging of those they love, and who inevitably will stand at the bedsides of their dying elders, trying to understand whatever final words, or silence, they hear.

James Lott
Staunton, Virginia
March 2007

The Pilgrim Path

Starting with Yes

THERE are stepping stones in our garden. They form a path through the perennial beds around a green bend of grass and into the woodland with its floor of matted leaves. Keene, our six-year-old grandson, helped me lay the stones, talking all the while about the bugs he found, the acorns on the ground, how worms were good for the garden, how Papa was going to build him a tree fort, and how a boy at school broke his tooth on the side of the bathtub. "He won't get another one until he's in the second grade."

It was a good day.

Keene has grown up now. He's taller than I am, and not particularly interested in tree forts. The stepping stones have settled into place, separating the walk into distinct segments. With each segment the garden changes. The sunshine perennials give way to azaleas; azaleas give way to shadowed ferns; ferns give way to lichen clinging to dead branches in the undergrowth.

The walk gives me a perspective on the garden, marking where I've been and where I'm going. It reminds me of Shakespeare's description of the seven stages of life, from the infant "mewling and puking in its nurse's arms" to the "whining schoolboy," and the lover, "sighing like a furnace," and finally to the aged one, "sans teeth, sans eyes, sans taste, sans everything" (William Shakespeare, *As You Like It*, Act II, scene 7, lines 142-149).

Like stepping-stones, the seven stages mark distinct segments of our path through life, and each segment leads inevitably to the next. We're moving through the sequence at varying rates, but the progression is universal. So, unless we die prematurely, we have no choice about entering old age. And old age brings with it a relentless series of losses—sight, energy, health, memory, touch that has the power to delight, friends who are dear to the heart. But, again, we have no choice. It's the next stepping-stone. It comes right after the one marked "late adulthood."

But we do have a choice as to *how* we enter old age. We can complain bitterly the way the Israelites did in the desert: "If only we had died by the hand of the Lord in the land of Egypt when we sat by the fleshpots and ate our fill of bread" (Exodus 16:3). Alternately, we can put a spin on the reality of our situation, and pretend that the older years truly are golden. We can dig in our heels and refuse to change our habits and expectations. After all, Peter Pan insisted, "I'll never grow up," so why can't we say, "I'll never grow old?" We do have some choices.

But to complain too much, or spin too wide, or refuse to change habits and expectations, can cause one to suffer what psychologists call "arrested development." No one wants to suffer "arrested development." It has a nasty, contradictory sound to it. Like our development got caught speeding on the interstate. And it renders one childish in a foolish sort of way. Hermann Hesse, in his essays on art and life, said, "A man who hates being old and gray, who fears the nearness of death, is no more worthy a representative of his stage of life than a strong young person who hates and tries to escape his profession and his daily tasks. . . . To fulfill the meaning of age . . . One must say yes to it."[1]

And if we refuse to say yes, eventually the winter rain will come, and there we'll be, standing out in the open, shivering with cold, "sans teeth, sans eyes, sans taste, sans everything."

So instead of seeing myself as a victim of old age, being swept down the path by unseen forces, I'd like to see myself and all my older friends for who we really are: a people diminished in strength, but still standing tall with the sun warm against our face. Given a choice as to how to enter old age, I choose entering it with a "yes."

And maybe even with hope. As Hermann Hesse said, "Old age is a stage in our lives, and like all other stages it has a face of its own, its own atmosphere and temperature, its own joys and miseries. We old white-haired folk, like all our younger human brothers, have a part to play that gives meaning to our lives, and even someone mortally ill and dying who can hardly be reached in his own bed by a cry from this world has his task, something important and necessary to accomplish. Being old is just as beautiful and holy a task as being young."[2]

Of course, that's not the way Sarah looked at it. There was nothing "beautiful" or "holy" in *her* life. She suffered the cultural shame of having never given Abraham a child, and "Abraham and Sarah were old, advanced in age; it had ceased to be with Sarah after the manner of women" (Genesis 18:11). So life was just leftovers—without meaning or purpose.

Then one day, in the heat of the afternoon, three strangers appear under the Oaks of Mamre. Abraham greets them and rushes back to the tent where Sarah is sitting, fanning herself with the Sunday paper. She wonders how long the strangers planned to stay. Abrahams says, "Make ready quickly three measures of choice flour, knead it, and make cakes" (Genesis 18:6).

Sarah does as she is told and just as she leans over to put the cakes in the oven, she hears one of the strangers say that she, a barren woman of ninety, would have a child. That definitely would not be good news for us in our old age. But it was for Sarah. If what the stranger said was true, she would be restored to dignity and her older years would have meaning and purpose. Sarah laughs at the absurdity of God's grace.

And so do we. We laugh with Sarah because the stranger's words promise that in the absurdity of God's grace being old will be just as beautiful and holy a task as being young. And even though we're approaching the end of the garden path, the ground beneath our feet is holy ground. Perhaps I'll take off my shoes the way Moses did. Then nothing—not even leather—will separate me from the One who taught me how to walk.

2

Rest and Remember

ON a path in Iona, overlooking the thirteenth-century abbey with its high Celtic crosses, there's a wooden bench. Someone donated it to the island so that pilgrims could sit down and enjoy a respite in their journey. On the back of the bench is a plaque that says "Rest and Remember."

So I did just that. After sloshing through bogs and climbing rocky knolls, I rested and remembered. Remembered St. Columba, how he sailed from Ireland to Iona in 563 AD and established a monastery on the island. Remembered the hermit's cell he built so he could find solitude for prayer:

> Lord, be a bright flame before me,
> be a guiding star above me,
> be a smooth path below me,
> be a kindly shepherd behind me,
> today and for evermore. Amen.[3]

But the more I warmed a bench on the distant shores of Scotland, the more I remembered people and events in my own backyard and how a "kindly shepherd" had led me to them. Remembered all the way back to when, like Dylan Thomas:

> . . . I was young and easy under the apple boughs
> About the lilting house and happy as the grass was green.
> . . .

Time let me hail and climb
Golden in the heydays of his eyes.[4]

Remembered what it was like when I first felt the nearness of
an adolescent boy. And how I married in a country church where
the heat dripped down my new husband's face until I gave him my
grandmother's lace handkerchief to use as a mop.

What it was like to have four children: Ethan, Matt, Kate,
Sally. How they crawled into my lap dragging their toys and books
until there wasn't room for any more. And how on the night their
father died we all slept on the bedroom floor—not wanting to dis-
turb the imprint of his head on the pillows.

What it was like trying to make ends meet. How we cheered
on the first day of the month when the Social Security check
arrived. "The eagle flew!" And Ethan said it was okay for me to
get a job teaching, but he didn't want me to work at Burger King.
I told him we shouldn't be too proud to work at Burger King. At
least, I think that's what I told him.

Remembered Sally asking if I could please find them another
father, and how Kate protested: "The good ones are already
taken." Then being introduced to a tall thin man from Minnesota
who told us about the boundary waters. How in the winter he
moved a little house out onto the frozen lake and drilled a fishing
hole in the ice. He and his father played cribbage by a stove while
they waited for the fish to bite.

Remembered being married at Easter time when the lilies were
still fresh and sweet smelling and how I whispered a thousand
thank-you's to the Lord, my God, who had peopled the earth with
faithful companions to lift us up when we stumbled. "How can I
repay the Lord for all his gifts to me?" (Psalm 116:12 NEB).

Remembered one of my students taking her own life, swal-
lowing a whole bottle of her mother's sleeping pills, leaving us to
grieve for the awful disillusionment of one so young. How her
dying made me wonder if I was meant to do more for those who
thought they were abandoned. Then going to seminary and finally
feeling the weight of a bishop's hands on my head, ordaining me
to carry the Gospel to the ends of the earth.

I didn't make it that far.

But I made it as far as Staunton, Virginia, a gracious town in the Shenandoah Valley. Remembered walking through the switchbacks and turns of parish ministry until it was the season to retire. Then going on a pilgrimage to Iona—not knowing exactly what I was seeking but trying to find answers to questions I had never asked. Then discovering that the pause to rest and remember was, perhaps, the most important part of the journey. It was T. S. Eliot's "still point of the turning world,"[5] where time present, past, and future were wound together in a circle of threads that looped and spiraled around each other. And there was a curious continuity in the pattern, as if it had been traced by the hand of an angel.

Rest and remember. What has been. What is and will be. I suppose you could call "bench warming" a Sabbath of the heart, which often, happily, leads to a nap.

3

Stepping Out

ACCORDING to tradition, King Solomon wrote the Song of Songs when he was a teenager. Life was full of possibility, and the king was enjoying his first flights of sensual bliss: "How much better is your love than wine; your lips distill nectar, my bride; honey and milk are under your tongue; the scent of your garments is like the scent of Lebanon" (Song of Solomon 4:10-11). The lines breathe a sweet eroticism which is probably why the church doesn't include them in the Sunday lectionary. They might tempt people to steal pew bibles and read them under the cover of night.

But the second book in the cycle, Proverbs, was written during Solomon's middle years, when the sun had arced across its zenith: "Keep sound wisdom and prudence, and they will be life for your soul and adornment for your neck; you will walk on your way securely and your foot will not stumble" (Proverbs 3:22-23).

Then, in the evening of life, he writes the book of Ecclesiastes. Naming himself as the philosopher king, Qoheleth, Solomon descends into a deep despair. He sees everything, including his cherished wisdom, as a travesty, "chasing after the wind" (Ecclesiastes 2:26).

"What do people gain from all the toil at which they toil under the sun? A generation goes, and a generation comes . . . the sun rises and the sun goes down. . . . All things are wearisome, more than one can express . . . there is nothing new under the sun" (Ecclesiastes 1:3-9).

The promise of achievement and self-advantage has withered. The sovereign will of God remains inscrutable. And there is nothing new under the sun. It's a very melancholy message, and you can't help wondering how the book ever made it into the canon.

Yet Walter Brueggemann says that the witness of Ecclesiastes is a necessary part of Israel's daring testimony. "There is within Israel an uneasiness about that marvelously positive testimony."[6] The uneasiness arises out of the wisdom of an aging philosopher king's retrospective vision, in which he sees the realities of life. And in the reality of life, God often seems absent: "for God is in heaven, and you upon earth" (Ecclesiastes 5:2). And God often seems unjust. "What happens to the fool will happen to me also; why then have I been so very wise?" (Ecclesiastes 2:14).

It's a countertestimony, and one that is troubling for many Christians, especially those who proclaim a marvelously positive gospel and an eternally smiling Jesus. But the more the sun descends into the evening of my life, the more that testimony seems to me to be authentic. And the more the sun descends into the evening of my life, the more I appreciate his uneasy witness.

I'm a bit uneasy myself. I have a linear yard of books on my shelf about surviving after sixty-five. They are full of marvelously positive testimonies like: "We're not getting older; we're getting better." The tone is one of cheerful, determined optimism. But it doesn't ring true.

It's sort of like the family picture on my desk. The cheerful demeanors don't ring true. Of course, I was the only one who wanted to have the picture taken. After all, we didn't get together that often so we might as well have a record of it—send it out in Christmas cards telling people how happy we were.

But did the family cooperate? No, indeed. First of all, they didn't bring clean white shirts to wear—claiming they didn't *own* any clean white shirts. (Which was probably true. My children have never heard of bleach.) Then when I tried to corral everyone around a picturesque setting, they complained. They wanted to have the picture taken *later* when they weren't so *busy*. And the little girls didn't want me to brush their hair, "It's fine, Oma. I brushed it this morning."

When we were finally ready and posed for posterity, we pretended to be happy. Smiles were plastered across our faces like Band-Aids. Only the baby offered a countertestimony. He was screaming.

And so I keep the picture on my desk just to remind me of the realities of life. We may pretend we're not getting older; we're getting better, but whenever we make such a claim, we'll hear a scream of protest. Sure, we're getting better in lots of ways. We can enjoy the benefits of leisure, freedom, a modest pension. There's less pushing, more waiting. Fulfillment is measured in qualitative, not quantitative, terms. All of that is better. But in the reality of life we *are* getting older. Even though the market tells us that we can reverse the process with wrinkle cream and plastic surgery, our outer natures are definitely wasting away. Aching joints are on a replacement schedule. Leftover collagen has lost the battle with skin that is no longer elastic. Flights of sensual bliss have "mellowed." Fading memories require post-it notes to be posted on post-it notes.

But what's even worse than fading memories is fading afternoons. They lapse into a deep melancholy—a listless depression, more than one can express. And in the reality of life, God appears to be absent: "My God, my God, why have you forsaken me?" (Psalm 22:1). On such occasions I understand why Solomon descended into deep despair. I understand what Emily Dickinson meant when she said: "There's a certain slant of light, / On winter afternoons, / That oppresses, like the weight / Of cathedral tunes."[7] I understand what C. S. Lewis meant when he said: "I hear a clock strike and some quality it always had before has gone out of the sound."[8]

The clock reminds me of the ultimate reality: we're going to die. It's the ultimate reality that Solomon finally had to face. "All are from dust and all turn to dust again" (Ecclesiastes 3:20). So it's no wonder he was disillusioned. After all, he claimed, in the wisdom of his middle years, that "you will walk on your way securely and your foot will not stumble." But death definitely makes you stumble.

And yet, in spite of reality's insistent authority, the core testimony in Hebrew Scripture remains positive. It proclaims with absolute joy:

My help comes from the Lord, who made heaven and earth.
He will not let your foot be moved: he who keeps Israel
   will not slumber.
He who keeps Israel will neither slumber nor sleep.
   (Psalm 121:3-4)

The countertestimony of Qoheleth doesn't erase that core testimony any more than the baby's scream erased his core testimony.
Like Qoheleth, he offered an authentic and necessary part of a testimony that everything in life isn't wonderful. But when the shut-
ter snapped and the baby was returned to his mother's arms, he
gathered his ragged breath and smiled. A real smile.

So maybe—just maybe—if I engage in honest contemplation
of debility and reality, if I try to remain open at once to grief and
possibility—just like Qoheleth and Solomon and our Lord Jesus—
I may discover that when I hit rock bottom, the rock is solid. That,
at least, is a faith with sustaining power.

And what's more, maybe—just maybe—I'll discover, as did
D. H. Lawrence, that beneath the countertestimony of "nothing
new under the sun" there's a core testimony of "*something* new
under the sun."

> As if, in the changing phases of man's life
> I fall in sickness and in misery
> my wrists seem broken and my heart seems dead
> and strength is gone, and my life is only
> the leavings of a life
>
> and still, among it all, snatches of lovely oblivion
> and snatches of renewal
> odd, wintry flowers upon the withered stem, yet
> new, strange flowers
> such as my life has not brought forth before, new
> blossoms of me—
>
> then I must know that still
> I am in the hands of the unknown God
> He is breaking me down to his new oblivion
> To send me forth on a new morning, a new man.[9]

4

Lost and Found

AS a child I often stayed with my grandmother in her apartment. There was a huge hall in the middle of the complex—wide enough for me to play jacks on the wood floor, or skip rope over the carpet. Sometimes I'd push a doll carriage around and around the stairwell, singing at the top of my lungs. "Swing low, Sweet Chaaaariot." But none of the neighbors complained—at least not until I decided to roller skate.

One day my grandmother told me to go downstairs and get the mail, which I did. Then I ran back upstairs and opened the door to her apartment. But standing in what I assumed to be her kitchen was a stranger. I had never seen the woman before. Where was my grandmother? I ran out and up to another floor but the same thing happened. A tall stranger was in my grandmother's kitchen. He looked down at me with dark and curious eyes.

By then I had blossomed into hysteria and had to be rescued by a neighbor who stepped out of her door and led me to safety. She knew where I belonged. But to this day, I can remember what it was like to be totally lost, without bearings, running through a wilderness of hallways.

And I still get lost. That's why I'd like to have one of those global positioning systems in my car. When I can't find my way, a nice lady comes on the speaker and says, "Turn right at the next corner and continue down Mountain Boulevard for one quarter of a mile." It's amazing. It's like having a guardian angel in the car.

And it's good to have a guardian angel when you're in your older years because you often feel lost in a world of worries. Where do I go from here? Will there be enough money for the whole journey? What happens if the pension is threatened? What about health care? And suppose I have a long-term illness; what would we do then? Or worse still, what if I have to wander through the hallways alone?

The uncertainties remind me of the way Dante felt when he entered the Inferno:

> When I had journeyed half of our life's way,
>   I found myself within a shadowed forest,
> for I had lost the path that does not stray
>   Ah, it is hard to speak of what it was,
> that savage forest, dense and difficult,
> which even in recall renews my fear.[10]

It's a terrible thing to find yourself in a shadowed forest. When it's two o'clock in the morning and the rest of the world is asleep, uncertainties evolve into anxieties. Anxieties evolve into fear. And, with all due respect, it doesn't do any good for someone to remind me of what Jesus said about the lilies of the field. I'm not a lily and that kind of advice only compounds the fears by making me feel guilty for being anxious.

So when I'm out of breath from running up and down the hallways of my mind, I close my eyes and pray for a good neighbor to step out of a door and lead me to safety. Sometimes being found is a lot better than finding. After all, the lost sheep didn't find the shepherd. The lost coin didn't find the housewife.

Our son got lost in the woods when he was a boy. He was probably following a trail that was more inviting than the one marked with blue paint. But we finally found him in the thicket sitting on a bed of dry leaves. He looked up, and reflecting the miracle of discovery, said, "Mom, Dad, I found you!" That's not exactly the way it happened. The boy had confused the grammar of life. It was only later—when he was no longer a child—that he learned about being found and how much better it was than finding.

So it was with Abraham. He and Sarah left Haran to journey down through the desert to Canaan. And in those days the desert wasn't considered a positive monastic experience. It was the dwelling place of demons, serpents, forces of darkness. And it was a terrible thing to be lost.

But one night when Abraham was lost in the world of worries—about God's faithfulness and the unfulfilled promise of a child—the Lord God appeared to him. "Do not be afraid," he said. "I am your shield and your reward shall be very great" (Genesis 15:1).

Then the Lord God invited Abraham to step outside his tent. "Look at the heavens," he said. And as his hand swept across the deep, the stars seemed to trail his fingertips, spreading out in a lacy train across the sky. "Can you count them?" he said. And Abraham, thinking that was what he was supposed to do, pointed to the heavens and started counting. One hundred and eighty-four. One hundred and eighty-five. One hundred and eighty-six. But the Lord God put his arm around Abraham's shoulder and whispered one word. "Infinity." So the two of them just stood there, side by side, gazing at the firmament. "Your descendents will be more numerous than the stars," said the Lord God.

Abraham was lost and then in the howling waste of the wilderness he was found. But not until he was lost. Perhaps some day when it's two o'clock in the morning and the rest of the world is asleep, I'll discover that being lost is the beginning of wisdom.

5

Like Trees Walking

R ETIREMENT feels a lot like crossing a finish line. The race is over. You can sit on the sidelines and watch others. Burn daylight. Breathe the useless air. Somehow, people at the office will manage to get along without you. They ask you to come back and visit, but that's exactly what they mean. Visit.

Finish lines can be very depressing.

But not long after I retired, I heard a familiar Gospel—about the blind man from Bethsaida. (My guess is that he was an old man with cataracts.) Jesus heals the man with the standard medical practice—spittle on the eyes and the laying on of hands. "Can you see anything?" he asks. And the blind man replies, "I can see people, but they look like trees, walking" (Mark 8:24). Oops. Jesus lays hands on him again, and the man sees everything clearly.

The story is Mark's introduction to a section in the Gospel on discipleship, and, certainly, discipleship requires us to see clearly. Not literally, but figuratively. Unfortunately, the disciples were often blind to what Jesus wanted them to understand about their mission. And we are often blind. That was the point of the sermon.

But what fascinated me about the Gospel was not its concept of discipleship, but the healing itself, particularly the midpoint. "I see people, but they look like trees, walking." It's an amazing image—like something out of *Fantasia*, or *Greek Mythology*. Halloween faces ballooning out of the trunks of trees. Daphne turning into a laurel tree to escape Apollo's ravishment.

I remembered reading C. S. Lewis's *Prince Caspian* and imagining the trees in Narnia that he described as looking strangely human. There were "pale birch girls . . . tossing their heads," and "willow-women" with long tresses hanging over their eyes. There were "queenly beeches," "lean and melancholy elms," "shaggy oak-men," and "shock-headed hollies."[11]

Maybe having partial sight was a good thing? Maybe it enabled the man from Bethsaida to see things more clearly—see what's hidden in the shadows of revelation, at the heart of paradox, which is God's very self.

I really should have been listening to the sermon. It was a good one—about the gradual formation of discipleship. The preacher was articulate, even a little passionate. But the Word of God reaches us where we are in life, and where I was that Sunday morning was on the other side of the finish line.

Finish lines can be very depressing.

Besides, as I remember, my hip was bothering me, and the air-conditioning didn't work. So I found it difficult to focus on developmental issues.

And I kept seeing those trees. Walking all over the place. Was there, perhaps, good news in the image itself? A kernel of truth hidden in the shadows? Emily Dickinson claimed that we should:

> Tell all the truth but tell it slant—
> Success in Circuit lies
> Too bright for our infirm Delight
> The Truth's superb surprise
> As Lightning to the Children eased
> With explanation kind
> The truth must dazzle gradually
> Or every man be blind—[12]

Was the "truth's superb surprise" a vision of the human condition for those of us who are moving into a new stage in life—where partial vision is a permanent affliction, even with trifocals? Was the blind man sending a message in a bottle washed up on the shore of our generation?

Looking out the windows of the church that morning, I could see cedar trees tossing their heavy garments in the wind, and I decided—right in the middle of the sermon—that the blind man from Bethsaida was a poet. Maybe even a prophet. As Abraham Heschel said: "Prophecy is poetry, and in poetry anything is possible, e.g., for the trees to celebrate a birthday."[13] The poet/prophet is endowed with an imaginative way of thinking and can therefore see a kernel of truth hidden in the shadows. For me, the kernel of truth was: we're a lot like trees.

When trees reach middle age, they stop growing taller and start getting fatter around the middle. Go figure. Their circulation weakens, and the topmost branches turn thin, even bald.

Some trees, like the aspens in Colorado, remain flexible in their old age. They bend with pressure, and even in an avalanche of troubles, they don't break. Good trees will continue to bear good fruit when they're full of years. And faithful aged ones will continue to lift up their branches to the light streaming down from heaven.

But what I really liked about the vision of the blind man is the fact that the trees were walking. They haven't settled down, anchored their roots, lost their vigor. They aren't sitting on the sidelines watching others in the game of life. They're walking.

In Narnia, trees move through the stillness as if in a country dance. And you can't tell whether they have feet or roots because, "when trees move they don't walk on the surface of the earth; they wade in it as we do in water."[14]

It's a vision that shatters all preconceptions about trees, and because of where I was that Sunday morning, with flights of inattentive fancy, it shattered all my preconceptions about retirement. People assume that when we cross the finish line, we're finished. But we're not. We're still walking. We may slow down a little, but we don't *settle down.*

After all, people like Michelangelo, Tolstoy, Verdi, Freud, Picasso, Churchill, and countless others accomplished their greatest works in their sixties, seventies, and eighties.

So, thanks to the blind visionary in Mark's Gospel, I now believe that we've been invited not only to remain as flexible as aspens, to bear good fruit, and lift up our branches to the light streaming down from heaven, but also to walk like trees. Perhaps, just move through the stillness of a country dance. Pickin' up our feet and puttin' 'em down. That's the gospel of the Lord.

6

Going Somewhere

MY grandfather's hands were old and soft and thin. I would often inspect them when we were at the dining room table. He'd be talking to the family about banks and loans and stuff, and I would sit next to him and try to push down the swollen veins that trailed from his wrists. It didn't work. They popped right back up again. I also tried to wipe away the nicotine stains between his fingers but that didn't work either.

Yet veins and stains notwithstanding, my grandfather's hands were good friends. When I was learning how to tie shoes, he wrapped them around my own and guided my fingers through the complexities of lacing. And, best of all, every day he and I went on a morning walk, hand in hand. Judge, the Chesapeake Bay retriever, went with us.

My grandfather called the walk his "constitutional." I never understood why he called it that since I had learned the meaning of the word in social studies. And walking didn't have anything to do with social studies. But the constitutional was always the same. He would strike out in long determined strides, gripping my hand in his own as if he were afraid of losing me. I'd quick step in order to keep up, while he talked about banks and loans and stuff, forgetting that I wasn't a grown up.

But by the time we reached Uncle Murray's house, he'd slow down a bit because he liked to inspect the fig trees and see if the fruit was dark enough to eat. Then we'd skirt the edge of the slough at the end of Battlebell Road. Judge would start trembling, thinking maybe there was a duck hiding in the tall grass. Finally we arrived at the railroad crossing. That was our destination. I'd put my ear down next to the steel track to see if I could hear a train coming, and my grandfather would take out his pocket watch to check the time. We threw out sticks for Judge to fetch, and then we walked home, hand in hand. There was always a cup of tea waiting for us, and an orange, cut so that the sections fell open in the dish like a flower.

That's what a constitutional was all about.

When my grandfather died, they crossed his hands over his chest. It rained that day. It rained a lot.

Now I am almost his age, musing about silly things like hands. But I think I have a better understanding of what a constitutional is all about. As a child, I thought it was solely to entertain me and the dog, but it was more than that. A constitutional shook the tension out of my grandfather's bones. It got the blood circulating, made necessary adjustments in his attitude. And if it was the season, it allowed him to taste the ripened figs, sweet with summer sun. That's what a constitutional was all about. And so today, if I can get all the movable parts of my body to cooperate with each other, I go walking in the morning.

By walking I mean walking, not running. I try to keep a moderately brisk pace because the doctor told me that it was good for the heart, and when I see young joggers on the same path, I move my arms up and down in a pretense of youthful energy.

But I like for my constitutional to have a destination. Treadmills bore me. So does the track around the football field that tempts people to clock how long it takes them to go nowhere. I prefer going somewhere. Maybe it's the memory of my grandfather's hands leading me to the railroad crossing. Or maybe it's just the instinct that prompts a pilgrim to put on a broad-brimmed hat, pick up a walking stick, and set foot on the path to a shrine.

The identity of the shrine isn't as important as the fact that there is one. It can be Santiago de Compostella, the hermit's cell on Iona, Bethlehem, Canterbury, Rome, Mecca, the sacred valley of the Incas, the Blue Mosque with minaret towers piercing the sky. It can be a stone chapel with shafts of dusty sunlight slipping through the clerestory. Or an old barn that opens its double doors to the sky. It can be the end of the driveway with a dilapidated mailbox and yesterday's newspaper wrapped in plastic. Whatever. There is a longing in the soul to go from—toward.

And maybe that's all we are conscious of—a longing, a deep restlessness in the soul.

There's a labyrinth in the floor of Chartres Cathedral, and in his book *The Art of Pilgrimage,* Phil Cousineau tells of meeting an old Frenchman there: "He tapped me on the arm with the crook of his oak walking cane. His were the eyes of a court jester, but bore the weariness of the wayward pilgrim. In deeply accented English, he asked me with the riddling power of a traveling bard, 'Do you know where I can find God?'"[15] Cousineau realizes he has been waiting for that question all his life, and he points over his shoulder to the black and white pattern on the floor.

I suppose that's the ultimate question: "Do you know where I can find God?" It would be good to follow the old Frenchman, through turns and switchbacks, uncoiling a thread of weariness until we reached the center.

But on some mornings I can only walk to the end of the driveway, or down to Wyants Store, where locals sit on the porch and talk about the storm coming in from the north. And yet, who knows, maybe on that short pilgrimage I will happen upon our Lord the way those two disciples did the afternoon they walked from Jerusalem—toward Emmaus. Imagine—they were talking *about* Jesus and then suddenly they were talking *with* Jesus. That would be nice.

So I'll keep taking my morning walk, searching the stranger's face. Then, having reached the railroad crossing, or Wyant's Store, or the end of the driveway, or wherever the shrine of the day may be, I can turn toward home.

And what a relief that is—to feel the ache in your knees, to see the hills roll away, and know that you are going from—toward home. It quickens the step and pulls you down the road—back where you belong.

I hope it will be the same on my last journey home. I hope that the valleys will be lifted up, the hills made low, the uneven ground made level, and the rough places, a plain. And I hope I find a cup of tea waiting for me, and an orange, cut so that the sections fall open in the dish like a flower.

The Crossroads

7

The Blessing of Weakness

BEFORE television, summer play lasted late into the evening. We played capture-the-flag and kick-the-can and hopscotch. The girls made necklaces out of clover leaves, and, invariably, the boys wrestled, pinning each other down and rolling over to escape the hammerlock. The one who thought he was the champion would insist that the other say "uncle." Give up.

And that's really what we have to do when we retire. We have to give up—give up power. We claim we don't have any, but we do. It's a power that most of the world's population has never imagined was possible to have—a power to influence people. It's vested in title, office, income, and authority. As for the church, no matter how "mutual the ministry," or how "integrated the authority," there's power in the Word. And when you're the one who carries the Word in your hands, holds it up in a leather limber bible, or proclaims it from a pulpit text, you're endowed with power.

I could feel it. I had ascended the stairs of the pulpit Sunday after Sunday, and there they'd be, some of them hugging the aisle, some in their "reserved seats" on the fourth row, epistle side, and some in the back where no one could see their little boy making paper airplanes out of the bulletin.

I knew where I could look for a bit of laughter, which eyes would easily fill with tears, and which ones would catch me if I rambled. "Bring it home, Sister." There they were, looking up at the pulpit as if I had an answer.

I'd often return to the sanctuary, long after the pews had settled back into place. There I'd kneel, and pray to be stripped of
any claims to power: "Not mine, O Lord, but thine." But usually,
within a few days, I could feel my head inflating like a hot air bal-
loon. I think I rather enjoyed the floating effect. I didn't want to
give it up.

And when you retire, it's not just power that you have to give
up; it's community—colleagues, consultants, office personnel,
friends who gather at the same well. I really didn't want to give
up my community. They were good people. They raised sheep,
taught school, listened for hours to operas, and sometimes fell
asleep during the second act. They signed for the deaf, delivered
meals, planted trees, wrote histories, repaired tractors. Together
we had learned to forgive and bless and laugh and sing and celebrate. How could I give all this up?

But I was tired. Some call it "compassion fatigue." And I was
getting old. My bones told me it was true. So did my driver's
license.

So do you accept or resist? Say "uncle" or roll over to escape
the hammerlock? The question is as old as time. It's the text of
religion, philosophy, politics. It's an issue with every human being,
from toddler to adolescent to adult, but it's particularly focused
when you reach a critical juncture in life, like retirement.

I wrestled with the decision for months, night after night, trying to pin down an answer, just the way Jacob tried to pin down
the mysterious stranger that night on the banks of the Jabbok
River. And just when I was about to drift back to sleep, the mysterious stranger would whisper in my ear, "You're getting old, and
down the road you might possibly have to give up . . . life itself."
There's the rub.

Jacob wrestled until dawn. And in a way, he prevailed. He
held the God/man in a hammerlock, and said, "I will not let you
go unless you bless me" (Genesis 32:26). Say "uncle." And Jacob,
the trickster, once again elicits a blessing. But it wasn't a blessing
of strength; it was a blessing of weakness. The stranger threw
Jacob's hip out of joint. He would limp into the future with an
arthritic reminder that God is God. But what a blessing that was.
And what a future there would be.

Jacob also received a new name. "You shall no longer be called Jacob, but Israel" (Genesis 32:28). In the ambiguity of a win/lose match, the new name signified a new person. I like that idea. They say that in India, when people pass from one stage of life to another, they often change their names. (I'm thinking of changing mine to Marguerite . . . or Tiffany.)

I don't know how I finally knew for sure that it was time. Maybe I saw the dawn break in streaks of light over the Jabbok River. Or, maybe I heard that earthly hum—deep in its resonance—that tells migrating birds when it's time to go home. Whatever. After months of wrestling I finally said "uncle," stood up, brushed the grass off my skirt, and announced my retirement. Then it was too late to change my mind.

We planned a ritual for my leave-taking. After all, we have rituals for life's other passages—baptism, bar mitzvah, graduation, marriage—so why not one for retirement? It's just as critical a juncture in life. We leave something behind that we can never go back to, anymore than we can go back to our college glee club or Saturday night at the bistro. And ritual has a way of voicing closure with words, music, movement, feasting, dancing. It kicks you out of one place and sends you sprawling across the floor to another.

We celebrated the Eucharist. And the end was a beginning because the service included the baptism of a child who was still blinking at the brightness of being. She received a new name. I returned the gifts of the church. "Receive this book and continue as persons of prayer." "Receive these keys and let the doors of this place be open to all people." Then we were blessed—our whole family—and dismissed. "Go in peace to love and serve the Lord."

There was a grand feast following the Grand Feast, with tables laden with chicken casseroles and gelatin salads and homemade breads. There were toasts and laughter and farewell gifts. And lots of memories. About the time the Christmas greens caught fire and Bart Hansen had to leap over the choir rail to put them out. And the time I tried to rope off the back pews, so the worship space wouldn't seem so cavernous and got slam dunked by the residents of the rear. They removed the ropes and wrapped them as a retirement gift. Lots of memories. About sputtering candles and fainting acolytes, and yard sales and parish picnics.

When it was over, I turned off the lights and started to lock the front doors, until I remembered that I no longer had keys to the church. Indeed, I was one of the few people in Augusta County who didn't have a key to that church.

They gave me the flowers from the altar and we drove away. It would be fun, retirement. Really nice. I could do all those things I never had time to do when I was working. Things like golf, and fishing, and travel. I could even learn the art of Asian cooking. Yes, it would be nice, really nice.

I had some leftover pound cake in my lap. It would last a few more days.

8

The Empty Nest

L AST spring I discovered a wren's nest in the garage. I was cleaning the flower bench and started to pick up a ceramic pot when the mother bird flew in my face. Then she streaked past me to a tree outside the door, where she took up an aggressive territorial song. I looked inside the pot and there, neatly assembled, was the nest with four mottled eggs.

Of course, I was respectful, and never touched the flower pot again. But occasionally I'd climb a ladder and peak over the edge to watch the incubation. The bird's head was barely visible in the cup of brown grasses. And ten days later I could see four wide yellow mouths. Both mother and father birds started flying in and out of the garage with bits of food in their slender beaks occasionally settling over the nest to brood.

Then the nestlings tried to fly. Stumbling to the ground at first, then winging it up to the trees. For several more weeks they flew around the garden, returning at frequent intervals with the obvious expectation of a big family meal. Then one day they were gone. No more fledglings. The nest was empty.

I finished cleaning the flower bench, which was much dirtier than it was before the wrens had taken up residence there. And whisking away the litter, I remembered cleaning up Matt's room after he left for college: there were lost socks under the bed, a broken ukulele, a ragged copy of *Catcher in the Rye*. There were torn blue jeans on the floor, sneakers wrapped in duct tape, and a shirt that said *Mary Poppins is a Junkie*.

Scattered in his closet were papers, books, posters, tin cans, gum wrappers, and bottle caps. There was Monopoly money in the desk and a few letters from teachers that had never been exposed to the light of parental eyes. There were stuffed animals—hidden in drawers lest his cool friends see that he still liked their companionship.

He had left in a hurry and I knew why. He was afraid I might say something outrageous like, "Good-bye, Son. Walk with God. Seek that which is good." And he would have been . . . "like, totally embarrassed." Besides, his eyes were prone to tears. They would well up when he saw Lassie in trouble or when he opened a Hallmark Christmas card. So, stepping off the porch, he gave me a quick hug and said, "Take care of my dog." Then, before I could grab him one more time, before I could straighten the collar of his shirt and run my hand across his uncombed head, he was gone. My son was gone. And college might as well have been the ends of the earth.

But I think the Spirit endows children in their high teens with the courage of Icarus. It manifests itself in protests and insurrection. "Curfew?! What do you mean a curfew? No one else has a curfew tonight!" It nudges them to get out of there. Leave. Ride their skateboards through downtown traffic.

Nudging is probably necessary because by then mothers and fathers (mostly mothers) have suffered a brain drain. With all their parental responsibilities—gathering, feeding, brooding, teaching—they actually think their children belong to them. It's *my* son, *my* daughter.

I read somewhere that the mother eagle is much wiser than the human variety. When it comes time for the fledglings to leave the nest, she'll actually begin to destroy the nest—picking up and flinging out the leaves and twigs and feathers that she has so carefully gathered. The young eagles look on, aghast. "What's she *doing*?!" But the mother pays no attention. She keeps on tearing apart their foundation. Eventually the nest is totally destroyed. And why? Mother eagles understand something that we often forget: Fledglings aren't meant to perch on the edge of a nest; they're meant to fly.

Of course, I've always marveled at the motherhood of Hannah. She never suffers a brain drain. But can you imagine? She gives up her son as soon as he is weaned. It was part of her vow. Like Sarah and Rebecca and Rachael, she was barren. And not only barren, she was tormented by the rival wife, Penninah, who paraded her fecundity for everyone to admire.

And, even though Hannah's husband, Elkanah, is quite loving, he doesn't get it. "Hannah, why do you weep? Why do you not eat? Why is your heart so sad? Am I not more to you than ten sons?" (1 Samuel 1:8).

Elkanah is so . . . *male*.

Barren and bereft, Hannah goes to the temple and prays. "O Lord of hosts, if only you will look on the misery of your servant and remember me, and not forget your servant, but will give to your servant a male child, then I will set him before you as a Nazirite until the day of his death" (1 Samuel 1:11). And the God of Israel, in the bounty of his grace, answers her prayer. A son is born and his name is Samuel.

Then comes the appointed day to return to the temple. Hannah stalls. "As soon as the child is weaned, I will bring him, that he may appear in the presence of the Lord, and remain there forever" (1 Samuel 1:22). If I had been Hannah, I think I would have played it loose with the contract. Like, are we talking about *weaned* in the literal sense or *weaned* in the figurative sense?

But Hannah is faithful to her vow. She seems to know that the child is not her own, that he came *through* her but not *from* her. So she gives up her son to Eli the priest.

I take great comfort in the fact that every year she made a linen robe for him—saying prayers of gratitude as she folded the hem a little longer than the previous year. I think that when she took the robe to the temple, Samuel was looking out one of the windows above the courtyard. She saw him.

Hannah's release of the child Samuel—like our own release of fledgling children—is a lot like professional retirement. And it's just as stressful. But as St. John of the Cross said: "How sad it is to see certain souls . . . which, because they cannot summon up courage to break with certain tastes, attachments or affections, never reach the harbour of perfect union. Yet it would cost them but a single vigorous flight to break the thread that holds them."[16]

And breaking the thread has its compensations. When life is no longer confined to a parental flower pot, we can fly. Not in and out of a garage, but way up in the sky—where we can watch the sunrise, feel the solitude of mile high silence, experience the ease of uncertainty, the grace of paradox, the strange truth of other ways. It's the kind of flying that's reserved for those who can be heedless of threats to the self.

And, of course, down the road there are other compensations. Take Naomi, for instance. In her old age she was blessed with the birth of a grandson, child to Ruth and Boaz. They named the child Obed, and all the women in the village came to see him.

"My, what a fine boy he is."

"And look . . . he'll be a fine man as well."

"Blessed be the Lord God of Israel for he has not left Naomi empty in her old age."

9

Holy Uselessness

ESTERDAY I was sorting through files in the attic and came across a curious note. It was from a teacher at Bright Beginnings where our grandson was enrolled, and the note said that on a particular day, in the fall of 1995, the children ate macaroni and cheese for lunch, and in the afternoon they "cooked red Jello and danced like leaves." Imagine—spending the afternoon in such spontaneous leisure. Twirling around under the autumn branches, catching the dappled light and laughter. Then later—when it was time for a snack—testing the red Jello with a finger to see if it jiggled.

It's child's play, of course, but in her book *Toward Holy Ground,* Margaret Guenther commends such activity: "We dare not let our inborn gift for play atrophy and wither away for lack of exercise . . . when we play we also celebrate holy uselessness."[17]

I've never heard "uselessness" described as "holy." On the contrary, I've heard it described as selfish, wasteful, bad. I suppose that's because the ideals of frugality and hard work were too deeply imbedded in my Protestant bones for me to consider anything holy except something that was "productive." But Guenther considers holy play and useless leisure to be the treasures of old age.

They are elusive treasures, however, especially in our sophisticated culture. Fifty years ago we thought Dick Tracy's wristwatch communication device was a crazy spin of cartoonist imagination, but now we have email, Palm Pilots, cell phones, and Blackberries. All these high tech toys are a boon for communication—allowing us to turn the living room into a virtual office. But when that happens, sacred leisure is crowded into a corner. And for lack of space, it atrophies, rendering us totally incapable of dancing like leaves.

You'd think that immediately upon retirement, we'd bring it out of the corner and embrace it like a long-lost cousin. But old habits are hard to change.

Besides, there's always a "to-do" list waiting for the retiree. The list may be spouse-imposed or self-imposed, but it has a purpose that goes beyond the overdue necessities, and that purpose is to make us feel needed. (Disengagement from the workplace can be traumatic for a psyche that's veiled in indispensability.) Included on the list are such things as cleaning out closets, caulking the bathtub, painting the kitchen, mending fences, etc., etc.

My list also included the enormous task of putting thousands of leftover photographs into scrapbooks. I had pictures of people I didn't even know. When I finally finished the to-do list, I began to enjoy the routine pleasures of housewifery—pressing fresh linens and stirring kettles of steaming soup. I even washed windows. But soon the windows were clean (or clean enough). The linen drawer was full, and there was enough soup in the freezer to last through two winters. I was uneasy. I knew the Lord God gathered the patriarchs into "eternal rest," but I sure hoped he didn't do the same thing to matriarchs.

Emily Dickinson, in a poem about the aftermath of death, speaks of "an awful leisure was, / Our faith to regulate."[18] The aftermath of retirement is similar in that it contains an absence—of routine, schedule, purpose, companionship. And as the months go by, we find ourselves avoiding the very leisure for which we yearned, lest an awful wave of loneliness pour into the abyss.

We take up vigorous sports, driving golf balls down a fairway, pumping weights, playing tennis. Some of us avoid leisure by traveling. I don't mean an occasional journey. I mean breathless travel, seeing all the sights there are to see—museums, mountains, monuments—seeing them not with the mind of a pilgrim, but with the mind of a crusader.

Perhaps if I'd been born a Jew, it would have been easier for me to enjoy occasional leisure. I would have grown up acknowledging Sabbath leisure as the habitual pattern of life.

"Remember the Sabbath day and keep it holy. Six days you shall labor and do all your work. But the seventh day is a Sabbath to the Lord your God; you shall not do any work—you, your son or your daughter. For in six days, the Lord made heaven and earth, the sea, and all that is in them, but rested the seventh day, therefore the Lord blessed the Sabbath day and consecrated it" (Exodus 20:8-11).

If I'd been born a Jew, I would've approached the "to-do" list with the same energy, but with a different attitude. I would have cooked and cleaned and polished and pressed with heightened anticipation—as if a queen were coming to live with us for the weekend. Then on Friday when the sun dipped below the horizon, I would have watched the kindling of candlelight. And I would've remembered how in the beginning God said, let there be light. And it was so. And God said let the waters separate and dry land appear. Let the land put forth plants with blossoms and fruit: azaleas and crepe myrtle, and lilacs. Bougainvillea, falling, pink as dawn, from staircase walls. Vines yielding tomatoes and beans and zucchini—lots of zucchini. God just couldn't get enough zucchini. Let animals roam through the forests. Let birds fly through the air—buntings with bright blue hoods and warblers with thin trilling voices. And let seals swim in the pools of salt water, rainbow trout in the streams of fresh water. And it was so. Then God created human beings, breathed into their nostrils the breath of life. With every day a new creation came into being. But at the end of the sixth day God rested—let the dew collect and bend the grass to sleep. It was good.

If I'd been born a Jew, I would've remembered all those stories. And I would've marveled at the beauty of it all. I also would've remembered what the ancient rabbis said: that at the end of the sixth day God had not quite finished his "to-do" list, because, even though creation was very good, there was something missing. The rabbis called that something *menuha*.

According to Abraham Heschel, "*Menuha*" means "much more than withdrawal from labor and exertion, more than freedom from toil, strain or activity of any kind. [It] is not a negative concept but something real and intrinsically positive. . . . To the biblical mind *menuha* is the same thing as happiness and stillness, as peace and harmony."[19]

And so God put the finishing touch on creation. And gave us *menuha*. And in a way, the seventh decade of life is like the seventh day of creation. It's the finishing touch. Having spent our productive years getting and spending resources, we settle down into being and absorbing *menuha*. Absorbing happiness, stillness, peace, and harmony.

Menuha. It calls for celebration. Maybe that's why the Sabbath morning prayer says, "He vested the day with beauty; / he called the Sabbath a delight."[20] And maybe that's why the Talmud tractate on marriage states that, "a righteous couple should make love every Friday night."

When Wayne Muller interviewed Jews with regard to that particular Sabbath injunction, he noted that: "One practitioner told me that it is traditional among some sects to make love four times during the Sabbath. Hearing this, I respectfully inquired as to whether he and his wife did, in fact, faithfully keep this particular precept. 'No, we make love only once. But,' he added with twinkle, 'we hold a deep intention for the other three.'"[21]

It may be a stretch for us to live the extended Sabbath of our retirement years according to the strict precepts of the Talmud tract. Indeed, it may even be a stretch for us to dance like leaves, given the problems we have with balance and everything, but we can at least hold a deep intention. And who knows what will happen on the seventh day of the week.

10

Fishing for Fish

SINCE I retired, I've switched from fishing for men and women, to fishing for fish. The technique isn't altogether different. We've never used the drag net approach in our church, which probably explains why we've never had a big catch. But, given my training in the minimalist form of evangelism, I thought I might possibly learn to fly fish.

I had watched my husband Denny do it for years. He was irresistibly drawn into the world of trout. It was where he was most at home—with the trees and the wind and the river and the fish.

I remember how we'd be walking along the side of Dunlap Creek, and all of a sudden he'd stop, and point to a place in midstream. "Look . . . beside the flat rock." And, sure enough, he'd have spotted a trout, its shadowy form holding steady in the current. We dared not move. Trout are skittish. And there's something about them that demands respect. Maybe because they are so ancient, so elusive. Or maybe because, no matter how much civilization encroaches on their habitat, they remain defiant in the face of extinction.

And I think our respect for creatures that struggle to survive grows deeper as we get older. When we are middle-aged, we get caught up in success, and security, and significance. And we have to prove our success, and security, and significance by having the best equipment and catching the most fish. Preferably big ones. Which is all very fine for the middle-agers. I wish them luck. Go get 'em. Bring home the lunkers.

But as you get older, your own life begins to appear as tenuous as the trout's, precariously balanced on the edge of oblivion. And fishing becomes something more than catching lunkers.

Gordon McQuarrie, editor of the Milwaukee Journal, wrote about his fishing father-in-law. He called him "Mr. President," and in his early life, Mr. President said, "I'm for picking out a trout so smart he thinks of running for the legislature."[22]

But then, as he grew older, he wasn't as anxious to pick out smart fish. One evening he climbed into the truck with McQuarrie and said, "Today . . . I may not catch a fish. No, sir. I may just get out in that there river and go along with it. It's the river I've been thinking about all the way down here—not the fish. . . . Somehow that river seems awful important today, whether there's a fish in it or not."[23]

The river is important to Denny as well. For him fishing isn't an escape from life. It's real life, beyond the artificial, a life that's immediate and intensified. The river whispers the gospel, proclaims the good news, invites him back into Eden for a few hours. Of course, he'd never use words like that to describe it. Fishing is fishing. But I could always count on it: early on a spring morning, Denny would look up at the sky, turn over his hand to feel the drizzle of rain, and tell me that he was thinking about going over to Dunlap Creek.

So we'd drive across Peter's Mountain to the side of the river. There he'd assemble his gear in a ritual sequence, and step out into the water to meet the fish, while I, untutored and undisciplined, still wrapped up in words, would settle against the trunk of a tree and watch him.

Standing tall and easy in his brown felt hat, he'd loop the line behind him, then unfurl it, lightly settling a fly on a seam in the current. It looked so easy, so full of grace. He'd cast again and again, following the drift downstream, sometimes reaching out to catch a mayfly rising off the river so he could match it to one on the brim of his hat. All the while he'd scope the water for a sign.

Then suddenly a trout would strike, leap out of the water— its supple body arching in a flash of silver. It would run for the cover of rocks and weeds—pulling against the line with an unyielding tenacity. Denny let it run and rest, run and rest, slowly working it into the shallows. There he'd ease the fly from the fish's mouth with the delicacy of a surgeon removing a splinter from the hand—sometimes kneeling beside the still water until the trout's gills stopped beating, and it slipped off into the river. Then Denny would begin again to fish for fish. It seemed as if he were picking up a rhythm that was deeper than his own.

And even though I knew the river was wild and unpredictable, I began to feel it tug against my own flesh. Clearly, Denny was onto something. And as long as I was just an observer, I remained outside of "something."

So I started reading books on "how to fish." Books explain everything. When the tip of the rod reaches ten o'clock, accelerate with a sharp snap. Stop at one o'clock. Momentum will carry the line back. Then reverse the movement. It looked pretty simple. I tried it with a weighted line in the front yard. Ten o'clock, snap, one o'clock, snap. At first the line only traveled about fifteen feet, curling up in front of me, like a mound of spaghetti. Denny said, "Relax. Let the line go when it's ready to go, not when you've decided to let it go."

"When *it's* ready? Like, who's in charge here? Me or the flimsy rod?" But after catching trees and tangling the tippet, I conceded to the flimsy rod. Training became more a process of unlearning than learning—with Denny coaching me in the manner of a good Zen master. We picked out dandelions for targets and I turned to watch the rod carry its weight behind me. Slowly, I began to feel when the line had reached its full length, and when it was time to let it fly to an imaginary fish in the grass.

I learned to tie flies to a gossamer thin tippet, willing my arthritic fingers to remember their nimble youth.

Then, one day, Denny said I was ready for the river. I wasn't so sure. Dandelions were one thing, but the river? It was cold, and often too dark to see beneath the surface. I remembered how Peter resisted when Jesus told him to put out into the deep. And how Nick Adams in Hemingway's *Big Two-Hearted River* was afraid that in the fast water, fishing would be tragic.

But there was no turning back. We drove over Peter's mountain, past houses waking up to day's labor, parked the car, and walked through the woods. Swales of new fern brushed against our ankles. Pine trees grew tall and straight with thin alleys of light coming through their branches. It was beautiful. I wanted to sing a doxology but I was afraid to break the silence.

Beyond us was the river moving through deep pools and strands of silver bubbles. I still didn't know if I was ready, but I put on the traditional dress—waders, belt, boots, chaps, hat. And a vest with an odd assortment of instruments hanging from its lapels. Plus a little box of flies in my pocket. Getting ready was almost . . . ceremonial. Like we were vesting for a liturgical procession or something.

Then we stepped into the river—bracing against its headlong rush until we could plant our feet on an island of silt and pebbles. Denny made the first cast, placing a fly near a spot where he had seen a dimple on the surface of the water. Then he gave the rod to me. I could feel his hand in the middle of my back. "Mend. Let it drift. Cast again." And so I did. Again and again.

I caught a few fish that day and in the months that followed—not lunkers but beautiful fish—browns with dark gold bellies and rainbows with "that red badge of courage along the lateral line."[24] The rod would suddenly come alive, pulling the fish closer to me, and pulling me closer to the river. Somehow it was awfully important to be close to the river. I was like a spy, smuggling myself into part of the Kingdom that could never be contained in the four walls of a church.

Then, when the shadows of evening had stretched across the water, I would once again settle against the trunk of a tree and watch Denny. Nothing else seemed to matter except the river and the presentation of the fly.

I suppose when I fold up my tent at the end of life, I'll reflect on what it was that brought me to a deeper faith in Christ, and I'll remember Dunlap Creek, the sycamore trees arching to midstream in a vaulted cathedral above my head. I'll remember the white-tailed swallows skimming the surface of the water. The sound of riffles and the music of the fishing line singing out its length.

And I'll remember the one who brought me there. Sometimes we draw closer to God simply because someone who knows and loves God takes us by the hand and leads us into the deep waters.

11

Fallow Land

THE months following retirement are full of uncertainty. It's an uneasy time. Like late August when summer vacation is wearing thin, and, except for a few pumpkins hidden beneath elephant leaves, there's no hint of the season yet to be. Flowers have gone to seed. The river has lost its momentum. Children kick up stones in the driveway and complain that there's nothing to do. Nothing to do. Even holy leisure takes on the stale taste of tedium.

Dr. Viktor E. Frankl, in his compelling study *Man's Search for Meaning,* addresses a far more serious feeling beneath the tedium—one "of which so many patients complain today, namely, the feeling of the total and ultimate meaninglessness of their lives. . . . They are haunted by the experience of their inner emptiness, a void within themselves; they are caught in the situation which I have called the 'existential vacuum.'"[25]

Frankl says the existential vacuum is widespread. "Let us consider, for instance, 'Sunday neurosis,' that kind of depression which afflicts people who become aware of the lack of content in their lives when the rush of the busy week is over and the void within themselves becomes manifest. Not a few cases of suicide can be traced back to this existential vacuum. Such widespread phenomena as depression, aggression and addiction are not understandable unless we recognize the existential vacuum underlying them. *This is also true of the crises of pensioners and aging people.*"[26]

I think the phenomenon is especially true of pensioners and aging people. Automation and electronics have eased the burden of late-life labor. Retirement homes have assumed more and more responsibility for our day-to-day care. And I'm grateful for all that. But when there's nothing to do, the existential vacuum grows deeper. And deeper.

It's tempting to leap into the breach with some heroic enterprise, preferably one with honor and a title (big mistake), or something so new that we fumble through it like awkward teenagers. I thought knitting would be a good way to fill the vacuum. I've always admired knitters. They seem so centered—as if their clicking needles gathered up all the raveled threads of care. It wasn't too difficult for me to learn the stitches, but, unfortunately, I never could figure out how to cast them off the needles. So the garment just grew longer and longer and longer.

I gave up knitting.

It's also tempting to leap into the breach with activities we learned in our youth. Tennis, anyone? But, as Jung said, "It is impossible to live through the evening of life in accordance with the programmes appropriate to the morning, since what had great importance then will have very little now, and the truth of the morning will be the error of the evening."[27]

Wanting to avoid errors of the evening, I decided to take some time out. I'd noticed quarterbacks giving signals for time-out during that endless season of football, and the signals set me wondering. Of course, the younger generation has co-opted the expression time-out as an idiom for parental discipline. (I have a grandson who's served more time-outs than a convicted felon.) But the primary definition of the word is derived from the world of sports, meaning the game stops so players can rest, confer, and adjust their strategy.

We're just like football players—sort of. We need to rest, confer, and adjust our strategies in life.

Of course, it could take a whole year to do that, in which case time-out would be more like fallow time: "When you enter the land that I am giving you, the land shall observe a Sabbath for the Lord. Six years you shall sow your field, and six years you shall prune your vineyard . . . but in the seventh year there shall be a Sabbath of complete rest, a Sabbath for the Lord: you shall not sow your field or prune your vineyard. You shall not reap the after growth of your harvest or gather the grapes of your unpruned vine: it shall be a year of complete rest for the land" (Leviticus 25:2b-7).

Our daughter Kate is a biologist and she told me that when the land lies fallow, the residue of plant and animal matter decomposes and releases carbon compounds for bacteria and fungi. Gradually, a nitrogen-rich humus accumulates in the soil.

Kate gave me more information than I needed, but what she seemed to be saying was that the process was one of re-creation. It prepares the land for new growth and new life. And the word "land" has a double focus. The first is on the good earth that produces a bountiful harvest. The second is on the dust of the ground out of which we were formed and to which we will return.

The dust of the ground, like the overcultivated earth, needs a rest. It needs to be nourished and replenished for the sake of new growth, new life, and a bountiful harvest. Jesus withdrew from the crowds, not for a Gatorade break, but because he was honoring a deeply spiritual need for rest.

So fallow time may be a good experience—even if it feels a little empty.

And the period of rest doesn't last forever anymore than time-out lasts forever. It's understood to be for a *limited* period—two minutes in football. (Two hours for my grandson.) Then the whistle blows and the game resumes.

Our game of life will resume as well. I'm sure of that. Soon there'll be something to *do* as well as something to *be*. And the existential vacuum will be filled to the brim with a love for our Lord Jesus Christ, a love that has been so nourished and replenished in the soil of our soul that a decision about *doing* no longer revolves around what or when or where. It revolves around Who.

In the meantime, I say kick off our shoes. Lean against a bale of hay. Listen to the crickets. Rest. Confer. Adjust. Pray.

Pray the way Thomas Merton did: "My Lord God, I have no idea where I am going, I do not see the road ahead of me, I cannot know for certain where it will end . . . and the fact that I think I am following your will does not mean that I am actually doing so. But I believe that the desire to please you does in fact please you."[28]

Hopefully, before long the road will rise up to meet us and we will be ready for new growth and a bountiful harvest. Then let the whistle blow and the game of life resume.

12

Second Careers

I RECENTLY met a retired naval officer who was a yo-yo man. He went from school to school teaching kids how to do "loop-the-loop" and "walk-the-dog." He could even make the yo-yo climb up the back of his leg. The children loved it. They begged to try the same thing. "Can I, please?"

The man seemed so comfortable doing what he was doing. After a career of leading men in the front wave of battle, he was content to put a string around his finger and spin a toy for the delight of school children. Opening their eyes to the potential of simple gifts like wood and string. And he was good at what he did.

Paul Tournier would probably say that the man had found a second career. While the chief motive of leisure—holy leisure—is pleasure, pure and simple, "A second career has a different motivation, one that is more social. It has a goal, a mission, and that implies organization, loyalty, and even priority over other more selfish pleasures."[29]

Second careers aren't as anxious or driven or rushed as the first ones, and the paycheck is often a plate of chocolate chip cookies. But there's meaning in the work. There's purpose and direction.

In Boynton Beach, Florida, a retiree at age ninety-five does regular duty at the police station reviewing stolen car reports. He no longer considers himself an *alte-kocker* (Yiddish for old timer) but an *alte-copper*. Would-be crooks in Boynton Beach are used to seeing old timers cruising through neighborhoods, their eyes peering over the steering wheels, their fingers ready to buzz for help if they spot trouble on the street.

Then there were Peter, Andrew, James, and John. Their first career was fishing. Their second . . . well, in their second career they did a little bit of everything. Paul was a tent maker, then a missioner. Jesus was an apprentice carpenter, then a healer, story-teller, grace-giver.

In Virginia Beach a group of seniors won a bronze medal for their award-winning wine. They had picked the grapes, crushed them, fermented the juice in a vat wrapped in an afghan, bottled the wine, and blasted on aluminum foil caps with a blow-dryer.

Second careers can be fun, especially when they involve a community. But they can also be difficult. Yo-yos get tangled. Dogs won't walk. Trouble threatens *alte-coppers*. Diseases infect the grapes and wasps attack them just as they're getting ripe and sweet.

But there's meaning in the work. There's purpose and direc-tion. And work that has meaning and purpose and direction can fill what Vicktor Frankl called the "existential vacuum" of older age.[30]

And yet there's a paradox here, because if the purpose of the second career is to fill the existential vacuum, it will fail. Frankl stressed the fact that "the true meaning of life is to be discovered in the world rather than within man or his own psyche, as though it were a closed system . . . being human always points, and is directed, to something or someone, other than oneself. . . . What is called self-actualization is not an attainable aim at all, for the simple reason that the more one would strive for it, the more he would miss it. In other words, self-actualization is possible only as a side-effect of self-transcendence."[31]

Self-transcendence. That has the whiff of gospel: "For those who want to save their life will lose it, and those who lose their life for my sake will save it" (Luke 9:24).

13

Here I Am

Some of my busy friends have a telephone service known as "call waiting." They pay money for it, and when there's a little ding-ding-ding on the line, they drop everything (including the conversation with me) to answer the other line. It's a model response to a call. They don't offer protests, as did certain prophets, to be just a dresser of sycamore trees or to have unclean lips. There's none of the disciples' hesitation: "I will follow you, Lord; but let me first say farewell to those at my home" (Luke 9:35). Like James and John, who left poor Zebedee in the boat, my busy friends leave me on a dead line with lots of unfinished nets to mend. It's a service with mixed benefits.

But my friends have a call waiting. That's what's important.

And I think we all have a call waiting—even in our older years. Of course, some folks think the "call" is only for the *ordained* ministry—for people up at the front of the church. That's a misconception that probably began in the fourth century, when Eusebius claimed that the Christian life had two characters, one devoted to prayer and the other to common life. It took the Reformation to correct his unfortunate notion. But even today people draw a distinction between the sacred and secular, the higher and lower, the *religious specialist* and the lay person.

They also draw a distinction between the young and the old, and assume that God calls only the young. As if the building of the Kingdom were a construction zone that required only the able-bodied. That's a misconception that probably began when someone suggested that the word *call* was synonymous with *profession* or *job*. And retirement meant not only the end of work, but the end of a vocation. At the farewell party, God gives the retiree a bronze plaque commending him for all his years of service, and that's the end of it. No job, no call.

Surely that's not the way it is. Too many of us still feel the tug at our sleeve, still hear the whisper at our ear: "Follow me." Sometimes we don't even sense our unique appointment until *after* we've retired. The job's distractions—salary, promotions, benefits, perks—make us deaf to the ding-ding-ding on the line.

Of course, as we get older, the call is usually modified to suit our limitations. It's not likely that God would send us to Nineveh, knowing how many rest stops we'd have to make along the way. The grand enterprises of life are behind us. And if we try to save the whole world, or become endlessly available to everyone, we'll just burn out before the first fruit appears on the tree.

I think vocations evolve as we get older. They become more modest in scope, but they also become more brilliant in focus, like a spotlight that contracts to a single beam on a forgotten leaf.

I knew a wonderful woman by the name of Mary Margaret who, at the age of ninety, took responsibility for tying bibs on the *really* old residents of her nursing home. Her back was so stooped with osteoporosis that she had to look up when she leaned over to speak to people. And yet every day at meal time she was in the dining room tying bibs and wishing the *really* old residents a good evening. Her call was modest, but brilliant in its focus.

And she wasn't the one who made the call. "You did not choose me but I chose you. And I appointed you to go and bear fruit, fruit that will last" (John 15:16). Mary Margaret was probably talking to her neighbor down the hall—about things like how Jimmy Phelps slipped on the ice and broke his hip, and how she didn't know what Louisa would do with Jimmy laid up and all. And how she hoped their grandson would straighten up and fly right.

And then all of a sudden Mary Margaret hears a ding-ding-ding. Call waiting. All she had to do was pick up the other line.

It's a hard concept to understand—the idea of a call waiting. Hard to accept the idea that we are at the other end of the line—

the receiving end. I'm so used to initiating projects—dialing the number and barging ahead with ideas.

I used to work at a Hispanic mission. The members didn't have a *real* church. No vaulted ceilings. No pews—just folding tin chairs in the living room of an old house. As resident aliens, they encountered countless barriers, and I had all sorts of ideas—good, solid Anglo ideas—to help them surmount the barriers. So I taught them how to *revision* with flip charts, focus groups, long-range plans, short-range plans. I even had medium-range plans just in case we had to move up the short ones.

I really had things going in that mission until one night I got there early for a meeting. I sat down in the living room on one of the folding chairs. It was a few days after Easter, and they had wrapped the wooden cross with tin foil to make it look special for the season. In a circle around the altar there were mason jars filled with jonquils. I could hear their voices—*Jesu Christo ha resusitado*—lingering like an antiphon in the living room, as if to block my willfully worthwhile path.

"This is my Son; my Chosen. Listen to him!" (Luke 9:35).

And yet, for most of us, it's hard to separate all the voices, especially when we move into the later stages of life. We may listen and we may hear, but whose voice is it anyway? The voice of culture? The voice of tradition? The voice of pride? Of habit? Of our own self-interest? Samuel heard the voice of God three times, but each time he thought it was the voice of Eli. "Then Eli perceived that the Lord was calling the boy" (1 Samuel 3:8).

J. Philip Newell, in his book on Celtic Christianity, speaks of the beloved disciple who leaned against Jesus at the Last Supper in order to listen for the heartbeat of God: "This spirituality lent itself to listening for God at the heart of life."[32]

But sometimes we don't even hear the ding-ding-ding, much less the heartbeat of God. We may only feel a restless spirit, a longing, or a curious sense of wonder about a current that seems to be pulling us deeper and deeper into unexplored waters.

And those unexplored waters may introduce us to the gifts which, I believe, are the particular manifestations of the Spirit in elders. Gifts like hospitality, compassion, understanding, laughter, wisdom. Maybe those are our gifts because we have survived youthful preoccupations with security and significance. We know about the sacrament of defeat. We're able to sit by firesides and bedsides. And when our friend next door calls with an invitation to play gin rummy, we say, "Sure." Because we know that it's not the game that matters; it's the company, especially on winter afternoons when there's no longer anyone to bring him a cup of tea. How fortunate that God sometimes calls us to play gin rummy with a friend next door.

And I believe our generation is a lot quicker to respond to such calls. We've reached a point in life where we don't have to weigh all the pros and cons. We have a call waiting, and, like my busy friends, we drop everything to answer the other line.

One of my favorite classic novels is *David Copperfield.* I read it often, and I always smile when I get to the chapter about Barkis. It's an early chapter in which a tearful Davy is sent away to school by his mean stepfather, Mr. Murdstone. But Barkis, the driver of the cart, has only gone a half a mile when suddenly he stops short. And out from behind the hedge jumps Davy's beloved nurse, Peggotty, who, being very plump and very affectionate, pops the buttons off the back of her dress whenever she gives Davy a good squeeze.

Peggotty doesn't say a word, but she takes the boy in both her arms and hugs him against her stays until Davy hears buttons rolling around the floor of the cart. Finally she releases him, stuffs his pockets with bags of pastries, and leaves. Davy cries again. Then he gives some of the pastries to Barkis. Barkis eats his share in one gulp. Then he casually inquires about the person of Peggotty. "Does *she* make 'em, now?"

> "Yes. She makes all our pastry, and does all our cooking."
>
> "Do she though?" said Mr. Barkis. He made up his mouth as if to whistle, but he didn't whistle. He sat looking at the horse's ears, as if he saw something new there; and sat so for a considerable time. . . .
>
> "Ah!" he said, slowly turning his eyes towards me. "Well, if you was writin' to her, p'raps you'd recollect to say that Barkis was willin'; would you?"
>
> "That Barkis is willing," I replied innocently. "Is that all the message?"
>
> "Ye—s," he said, considering. "Ye—es; Barkis is willin'."[33]

Barkis obviously has "intentions," and they're not exactly self-less, but he puts no conditions on his willingness. His response is open-ended and absolute. "Here I am." He's willin' to follow Peggotty whenever and wherever. Just say the word.

Perhaps when we're "willin'," when we've held the hands of the bereaved, and played gin rummy with our friend next door, we'll realize that we were called into the Kingdom for just such moments as those.

A
Slower
Pace

14

The Sky's the Limit

L AST year we gathered sisters, brothers, uncles, cousins, and a few etceteras for a family reunion. It was an early November day, and even though the grass was burnt with frost, the air was warm and windless. We played lots of games—football, tug-o-war, sack races. We ate heaps of North Carolina barbecue and tried to settle arguments about who won and who lost. Finally, when the competitions were exhausted, we went over to the community hall where we danced to a fiddler's tunes.

Just outside the window, on a hill overlooking Pigeon Top Mountain, the moon began to rise. It was round and full. But at the end of the second hour a shadow crossed its surface.

Knowing what was about to happen, I lifted Jack, the youngest child, up in my arms and walked outside. There we watched as the face of the moon was fully eclipsed. Jack, who was very impressed with the day's activities, turned to me in amazement. "Oma," he said, "how did you do that?"

It was great to bask in the warmth of Jack's wonder. But I had to admit that I wasn't wholly responsible for the eclipse. There are limits, the faith of a child notwithstanding. And lately, I've had to admit that the measure of those limits is shrinking. One day we wake up and realize that we can reach out and touch the walls on either side of us. There's barely room to turn around. And the limitless possibilities of human reason, memory, sight, willpower, energy, grit, and sheer determination are gone. It's a rude awakening. Ironically, it's often the first time we glimpse what it may have been like for an eternal, infinite God to be encased in a baby's skin and the limits of mortality.

But it's hard to accept limits. If we can create a wireless network, why can't we do just about anything? We hear the voice of deception whispering in our ear, "Go ahead. Try it. You can still hit the ball across the water with a seven iron. You can ride a surf board. You can fit into a size ten. You can wear high-heeled shoes, you know, the ones with pointed toes and red leather straps around the heel."

They say real soul-making doesn't begin until we can turn our backs on such temptations.

I think real soul-making began for Peter that time on the Sea of Galilee. He was moving into old age about then. (At least, that's the way I imagine him because in all the icons his hair is a mass of gray curls.) A huge storm was tossing his boat about when suddenly, out of the luminous darkness, Jesus appeared, his robes flowing full in the wind. And he was walking on the water, skimming along as if the surface tension were all he needed to sustain his purpose.

Peter was amazed. "How did you do that?" He asked if he could try to walk on water and Jesus consented. So Peter climbed out of the boat and started walking toward Jesus. Slowly. One step at a time, holding out his arms as if he were on a balance beam. Then he looked down at the waves. Big mistake. The foundation beneath his feet collapsed. He cried out, "Jesus, save me!" Of course, Jesus did save him, reached out his hand, and caught him by the scruff of his neck right before he sank. "You of little faith," he said. And the storm ceased (Matthew 14:31).

I love that story. Whenever it's Matthew's turn to proclaim the gospel, I listen with an anxious heart, knowing how cold and ruthless the waters can be. Then I settle back in the pew and wait for the preacher to tell me how I need to step out in faith, just like Peter, but how I have to keep my eyes on Jesus, not the roiling waves, and how, no matter what, Jesus will not let me sink into the deep.

It's an altogether satisfying message and, as I leave church, I'm determined that, beginning Monday morning, I'm going to have a lot more faith.

But the last time I heard the story, I remembered a road sign I used to see when, as a child, we motored through the mountains of North Carolina and Tennessee. It said "Jesus Saves." And I wanted to know *what* Jesus saved. Coins? Stamps? Shells from the Sea of Galilee? I asked my mother what it meant, but she said not to worry. "Episcopalians don't say that." So I finally concluded that there was no object to the verb, that Jesus was just naturally frugal.

But I think I've finally found the answer to the question. What does Jesus save? He saves old fools. And I think he consented to Peter's request to step out of the boat because he wanted the disciple to see that it was foolish, presumptuous even, to try to be more than he was, which was not only human, but old human. There are limits. If Peter had developed more than a little faith, he would have stayed in the boat and let Jesus come to him. He would have lived into the psalm:

> O Lord, my heart is not lifted up,
> my eyes are not raised too high,
> I do not occupy myself with things too great and too
>   marvelous for me.
> But I have calmed and quieted my soul,
> like a weaned child with its mother.
> My soul is like the weaned child that is with me.
>   (Psalm 131:1-2)

I hope when I'm tossed about by huge storms, I don't try walking on water. I hope I stay right there in the flat-bottomed boat. And, perhaps, someday I'll see a vision just like Peter's, of our Lord walking toward me, his robes flowing full in the wind, his hand reaching out to gather me up into the luminous darkness.

It's a vision worth waiting for.

15

Triple Sight

MY father wore bifocals. The reading lenses were outlined in boxes on the glass, and if he wanted to inspect
something, he'd tilt back his head and peer down
through the boxes. Sometimes he tried to inspect my face for
smudges or adolescent blemishes, but I dodged him by tilting
back *my* head. We never spoke of this cat-and-mouse game, and
by the time he was in his seventies his eyes were clouded with
cataracts. There was a deeper curiosity in his eyes, as if he
wanted to capture and print the memory of a face on his retina.
Then the sharp edges of the world began to soften. He'd lie in
bed for hours and watch the veil of rain sweep across the sky.
And then the windows closed.

I don't know how many months it took for me to get used to
the empty bed in his room. The spread was disturbingly neat.

And I don't know how many months it took for me to realize that *my* vision, as if on cue, had suddenly weakened. I was
forty at the time, and they say that's when the windows start to
fail. I bought a pair of bifocals.

At first the boxes were outlined on the glass, just like my
father's, but now they are fashionably blended, and only a slight
tilt of the head reveals my intention to inspect. I inspect the details
of life, the minutia, the infinitesimal. I inspect paintings—peering
down through the lower lenses at brushstrokes. (The museum
guards politely remind me not to get too close.)

But lately I've noticed that I *have* to get close in order to see. And my distant vision has weakened as well. Take street signs, for instance. I search for their names, but sometimes I can't see them until I'm on top of them. Then I have to brake suddenly. That upsets drivers behind me. (They aren't as polite as the museum guards.)

Sight is precious. And it's a bitter thing not to be able to see brushstrokes and street signs. The poet, John Milton, lost his sight when he was still a young man. He describes the pain of living in darkness in a poem called "On His Blindness:"

> When I consider how my light is spent,
> Ere half my days, in this dark world and wide,
> And that one talent which is death to hide,
> Lodged with me useless, though my soul more bent
> To serve therewith my Maker, and present
> My true account, lest He returning chide,
> Doth God exact day-labor, light denied?[34]

Of course, the poet's "one talent which is death to hide" was not lodged with him useless. He went on to write *Paradise Lost*. And he claimed that during the years of its composition, even though he was blind, he could see light in the darkness. That's important. I think, as elders, we can adjust our bifocals in order to inspect the details in life and search for street signs, but total darkness? That's a tragic situation.

Years ago there was a huge ice storm in Virginia, causing a loss of power for days. We could hear the limbs of trees scratching against the window panes, but at night we could see nothing. There was total darkness. It was even worse down in Tennessee where our daughter Kate was in school. But Kate and her friends, who took great pleasure in any adversity that canceled classes, invented ways to find light in the darkness. At first they used battery-powered flashlights, and when the batteries failed, they "borrowed" some votive candles from the chapel.

Hearing of their situation, I imagined them as biblical brides-maids, with lanterns in their outstretched hands, following the groom to the wedding feast. But that was not exactly their method. As Kate explained, "If you carry a candle in your hand, how are you going to carry your books and coffee cup?" So Kate and friends put the votives on the toes of their boots. "Melt a little wax and they'll stick," Kate assured me. Then they wandered through the darkness, with flickering lights dancing off their boots.

I keep the image of those wise women in my mind for the day when the sharp images of my world begin to soften. When that happens, I'll borrow some votive candles for myself and all the friends I have who suffer from cataracts and glaucoma and macular degeneration.

I'll also keep in mind the image of Bartimaeus, the beggar who sat by the side of the road, eating the dust of travelers. He was blind, but he could see that the stranger from Nazareth, walking between Jericho and Jerusalem, was Jesus, son of David—a light shining in the darkness. Often, as Keats says in his tribute to the blind Homer, when one cannot see, a curtain is rent in two and all of Heaven is revealed.

"There is a budding morrow in midnight;
There is triple sight in blindness keen."[35]

Maybe Paul, on the road to Damascus, was *struck* blind so he could see the same thing. As he says in Corinthians: "We look not at what can be seen but at what cannot be seen; for what can be seen is temporary, but what cannot be seen is eternal"(2 Corinthians 4:18). That's also why Moses spoke out so boldly. He had been summoned to the mountaintop. There the Lord God started telling him how he was going to liberate the Hebrew people. And Moses interrupted: "Show me your glory." I think it was a bit presumptuous of him, and he only got to see the *backside* of glory, but he knew that what could not be seen was eternal.

Above my desk, there's an icon of the Sinai Christ, the Pantocrator, wrapped in dark robes, lifting his hand in a blessing. The figure is pushed forward toward me, as if I were important or something. It's less a portrait than a presence, and, gazing at it, you get the feeling that you're looking at something beyond the visible.

So maybe when we old folks are summoned to the mountain top, we can all go up together, arm-in-arm. Peering through our mutual lenses, searching, stumbling, braking, gazing. We can wander through the darkness, with flickering lights dancing off our boots. And laugh to see that the darkness isn't dark at all. Then when we get to the top we can turn in our bifocals for a glimpse of what cannot be seen.

16

Original Joy

I ONCE heard a story about the first year that Adam and Eve
spent in the east of Eden. William H. Muehl, Clement Profes-
sor of Christian Methods at Yale Divinity School, told the story
in his inimitable style, and however apocryphal the story might be,
it shows that the Fall possibly was fortunate. The story went
something like this:

Adam and Eve—rejected, guilty, ashamed—searched far and
wide for a place to settle down. Some places were too windy, some
too cold, some too dry. Finally they found a stretch of bottom land
near the Jackson River where they could plant a field of wheat.
Adam fashioned a plow out of scrap iron and hitched it to a mule.
The soil was rich and turned easily in dark furrows beneath the
blade. There weren't many rocks either, although Adam had half
expected to run into lots of them, given the sentence the Lord God
had pronounced upon the land: "Cursed is the ground because of
you; in toil you shall eat of it all the days of your life" (Genesis 3:17).

Of course, it was hot; gnats swarmed around his head, and he
had to mop his face to keep the sweat out of his eyes. But at mid-
day Eve brought him a meatloaf sandwich and a pitcher of pre-
sweetened ice tea. Then, when the sun dipped behind the hill,
Adam put the plow away in the barn and pulled off his boots. His
back was tired, and there were blisters on his hands, but it had
been a good day, a really good day.

He and Eve sat on the porch steps looking out over the land
and marveled at how fortunate they were. Adam said, "Eve, God

was wrong! I mean, Eden was great, I'm not knocking it—it was wonderful having everything we wanted—but *this* is what we were meant for: to work, fail, try again, feel your muscles ache at the end of the day, but to know that what you had done with your hands was good. Really good." And somewhere between the distant stars and the breath of Adam's words, God heard the young man speak, and, hearing, God smiled.

In the ambiguity of God's providence, Adam had discovered the redeeming grace of manual labor. It was a discovery that, as Esther de Waal points out, St. Benedict would remember many years later: "St. Benedict insisted that since body, mind, and spirit together make up the whole person the daily pattern of life in the monastery should involve time for prayer, time for study and time for manual work."[36] In Benedictine orders, six hours a day are devoted to the work of the hands in domestic chores and the management of the land. As de Waal explains, "work with the hands can give something which is not found in dealing with papers, making plans, sitting on committees. The very act of touching, handling, feeling material things helps to build a small barrier against the torrent of words, written and spoken, which threaten to monopolize us by insisting that they alone constitute reality."[37]

There's a Cistercian monastery across the river from us. It's called the Monastery of Our Lady of the Angels, and the nuns (I call *them* the angels because their faces seem to be eternally young) seek a contemplative lifestyle in a "school of love." But they balance their life of prayer and study with manual labor—making Gouda cheese. You can taste and see that the cheese is good.

But for most of us it is difficult to maintain a balanced life. We're caught up in the torrent of words, written and spoken, and the work of the hands is all too often restricted to a keyboard.

It was easier in the "olden days" when we were young and newly married because the home demanded at least six hours of work a day. There was the garden that had to be planted, weeded, watered, and picked. You had to bury the spuds, mound the squash, stake the beans. And when it was harvest time, there was canning, pickling, and preserving to be done.

Then there was laundry. I was lucky enough to have a washer when we were first married, but it was years before I had a dryer. So I hung the wash out on a line in the back yard, pulling clothes pins out of apron pockets. And if it threatened rain, I'd gather the whole wash up in my arms and run for shelter.

Over the years, things got easier. You could buy preserves for $1.79 a pint. With the purchase of a dryer and the advent of polyester, all we had to do was fold the clean clothes. And fold and fold. I actually think that when it got easier to do laundry, we did more laundry. Maybe our hands were longing to smooth out wrinkles, and press seams in the long-legged jeans.

Then there was the dishwasher. And by the time the kids grew up and moved away, there were no more cuffs to take up or hems to let down. Just a little mending in the basket. Labor became more head work than hand work.

But something was lost. As the need for manual labor declined, the spirit seemed to be disembodied, flapping like empty laundry on the line.

It was probably about that time that I joined the church's Altar Guild. Perhaps because of an unconscious impulse to "build a small barrier against the torrent of words." The women on the Altar Guild prepared the holy table with such reverence. They polished brass, arranged flowers, changed linens—as if work were a prayer. Their hands were consecrated. Like those of Ruth, the Moabite, who gleaned the rows of barley, and Boaz who threshed it. Like those of the craftsmen who built the Ark of the Covenant out of acacia wood. And the Baptist who poured water over the heads of sinners. Like those of Martha who worked so hard in the kitchen. And Mary who anointed Jesus' feet with costly perfume and wiped them dry with her hair. Like those of the Creator who molded us out of clay on a potter's wheel.

Esther de Waal quotes a Celtic bard whose labor of the hands brought a song of praise to his lips:

Bless O God my little cow
    Bless O God my desire;
Bless Thou my partnership
    And the milking of my hands, O God.

Bless O God each teat
   Bless O God each finger;
Bless Thou each drop
   That goes into my pitcher, O God.[38]

Paul Tournier says, "It is a matter of the deep springs on which one draws. Ploughing and sowing, milking, building, sewing and cooking have always been . . . the primitive gestures by which man has manifested his humanity. . . . [The] original joy remains inscribed in that sub-soil of the mind which Jung called the collective unconscious. It is set vibrating once more when he performs those gestures again."[39]

Original joy—it's worth recovering. I think Denny and I were trying to recover it when we planted our vineyard. Like a garden, a vineyard requires manual labor from early spring to late fall— pruning, spraying, weeding, and trimming. We usually harvest at dawn on a morning in late September when the birds hover over the vines, signaling that the grapes are ready. Harvesting is heavy work. It makes your muscles ache, but, like the apocryphal Adam, when the sun dips over the hill and you finally sit down on the porch steps, you can say that it was a good day, a really good day.

But there'll come another day in the not too distant future when I can no longer be a laborer in the vineyard. The bursitis will get worse. Bending over will become hazardous, and my hands will lose their dexterity. Then what? People tell older folks to sit down and not worry about the chores. But we can't afford to do that! We *can't* quit, no matter what. We *can't* give up that original joy.

So I'll hang in there as long as possible even if my knuckles are swollen and all I can do is menial work. I'll teach my grandchildren how to make biscuits. I'll invite them to sit beside me and shell peas into a tin bowl. And when the bowl is full, they can dig their hands into the mound and let the peas roll off their fingertips. Plinkplinkplinkplink. I'll tell them that their work is holy. That it sanctifies the ordinary. Of course, they won't understand what I'm talking about, but maybe one day, when their lives are overwhelmed with words, they'll remember what it was like to hold in their hands a shell's worth of cool green peas.

17

Tied with Silver Cords

THERE'S a definite difference in pace when you compare the young and the old. The young are always in a hurry. They don't even stop at street corners and wait for the light to signal the walking green man. "My perception now is that the young seem always to be running (even though they are walking)," says Donald X. Burt. "They run to 'work out' (though they don't need to). They run to 'party' (celebrating their stamina, I suppose). They run to eat fast food so that they can run even faster. They pretend to be 'cool' but to me they seem quite steamy—hot with excitement about so many things to do and so many events to experience. They seem ever to be in need of a cold shower."[40]

I don't understand all the rush, but the truth is, I envy young people. I walk so slowly these days, especially when I go up stairs. If I could run the way they do, I could experience so many events: plays, exhibits, classes, concerts, sports, feasts, games. There would be so many things to do.

And I not only envy the way young people run. I envy the way they look. They're all so handsome. Their faces are smooth as creek stones. Their arms are round and strong. And their bellies are flat.

My friends say "I wouldn't be their age again for love nor money." I agree. I wouldn't be their age again either. I'd just like to have some of their stamina. And their flat bellies. Now and then envy tempts me to turn back the clock with a few nips and tucks, lasers, lotions, potions, and peels. Then I remember Aesop's fable—the one called *The Swallow and the Other Birds*. It warns against letting the seeds of evil (as in envy) grow. According to the fable, a countryman was sowing some hemp in the fields and a swallow warns other birds in the area to pick every one of the seeds off the ground. The birds pay no attention, and, of course, the hemp grows. The countryman cuts it and twists it into cords. Then out of the cords he makes nets in which he catches many a bird that had not heeded the swallow's advice. At the bottom of the page Aesop adds a moral in case we didn't get the point of the story. The moral is: we should destroy the seeds of evil before they grow up to our ruin.

King Saul had not read Aesop's fable. The seed of envy was planted in his heart when he first saw young David. "And whenever the evil spirit from God came upon Saul, David took the lyre and played it with his hand" (1 Samuel 16:23). He soothed the stormy king. But when king and warrior returned from a battle with the Philistines, "The women came out of all the towns of Israel, singing and dancing, to meet King Saul, with tambourines, with songs of joy, and with musical instruments. And the women sang to one another as they made merry, 'Saul has killed his thousands, and David his ten thousands" (1 Samuel 18:6-7). Saul hears the song and the seed of envy grows up to his ruin. In a jealous rage he tries to pin the young warrior to the wall with a spear. Ultimately Saul dies on his own sword.

It's a tragic story. And the older I get the more sympathy I have for the pathetic old king. I suppose if he had lived in the introspective culture of the West, he might have realized that his envy was a secondary emotion. Once he peeled back the bark and took away the wounds of time, ring by ring, he would have discovered, beneath the envy, a muted sense of helplessness and fear. Looking at young David with his round strong arms and the dancing women with their faces smooth as creek stones, Saul would have realized that he, the King of Israel, was a lot closer to the time to die than he was to the time to be born. And seeing the discrepancy of age, he might have understood that it was the Great Destroyer that rendered him helpless and fearful. That revelation occurred to Dylan Thomas at an early age:

The force that through the green fuse drives the flower
Drives my green age; that blasts the roots of trees
Is my destroyer.
And I am dumb to tell the crooked rose
My youth is bent by the same wintry fever.[41]

I suppose each of us is a little envious of the fact that young people are closer to the time to be born than they are to the time to die, but I hope that when I cross over to the other side, I remember to look back and tell the ones behind me not to be afraid. That even though the crooked rose will die, in the spring of the year it will bloom again. And its blossoms will be gathered up, tied with silver cords, and carried into the mansion. I'm sure of that.

In the meantime, I'll pray. "From malice, envy, and hatred, good Lord, deliver us." And I'll try some of that "age defying cream" I saw advertised in a magazine at the dentist's office.

I'll also think about the possibility that David might have envied Saul. It's a comforting thought. After all, scripture says, "There was not a man among the people of Israel more handsome than Saul; he stood head and shoulders above everyone else" (1 Samuel 9:2). And envy, which manifests itself at every age, is usually directed at someone *older*. The four-year-old envies the six-year-old because he gets to go to school and carry a really cool backpack. The ten-year-old envies the sixteen-year-old because she can pierce her ears and wear eye makeup. The sixteen-year-old envies the twenty-year-old because he can drive with his buddies across the country in an old beat-up van. The twenty-year-old envies the thirty-year old because she has finally found someone who accepts her for who she really is. So it goes from age to age.

One afternoon, years ago, when I was still running between appointments and meetings, I went to visit an older parishioner. She was sitting in a chair near the window. "What a surprise," she said and reached out to take my hands. Puffs of white curls framed cheeks that were pink and plump as a child's. Her glasses rested on the end of her nose, and in her lap was the tatting she always worked on. Leaning closer to the window where the afternoon light was slanting across her shoulder, she picked up the tatting and started drawing the cotton threads in a circle of loops and twists and spirals. It was hypnotic—the motion of her hands and the melody of her voice. We had some tea with cinnamon toast. I wanted to stay there for a few more hours—maybe until the light faded in the window and it was time for supper. Something like envy grew up in my heart.

Looking back on that day, I can imagine others feeling the way I did. Wanting to sit with some needlework instead of going to another meeting. That's why lately, when young people hurry past me on the street, I lift my hand in a royal gesture of greeting, nodding to the left and to the right, mentally offering advice: "Enjoy the day. Keep on running. And don't let your envy grow too tall. Someday, if you're lucky, you'll arrive. Then you can sit down by a window, create designs in a circle of loops and twists and spirals, and have a cup of tea with cinnamon toast."

18

Emptiness of Being

WHEN we moved from our first home, the biggest problem we faced was getting rid of things. It's amazing how quickly stuff collects, and when you live in a house for ten or twenty years, it *really* collects, especially in the basement. If you don't know what to do with something, take it to the basement. There's always room for more.

As for the children, they never threw anything away. Kindergarten art was still on their shelves. So Denny gave each of them a green garbage bag. "If you can fill this up by Friday night," he said, "I'll take you to Burger King." It was a game. All week long they collected junk and threw it into their garbage bags. And if a territorial boundary was crossed, it drew a sharp response. "That's *my* junk!" But, bit by bit, the rooms were cleared of clutter, and plates were filled with Whoppers.

Ethan was very proud of his achievement. Lying on his bunk one afternoon, he surveyed all the empty space with preteen pleasure. It held such promise for him. "Now I've got room for lots more things." That wasn't exactly the point, but it was exactly the way it was. We moved and the new shelves collected more stuff. So did the basement.

Why do we let that happen? I suppose it's primarily sloth, and yet I've often seen really strong resistance to getting rid of things. Especially in older folks. We arrive at a critical juncture in life, and it's time to "downsize." But we're reluctant to let go of things, useless things, like broken hair dryers. "Maybe I can fix it." The object in the discard pile seems freighted with historical meaning. The last time I moved, my sister had to pry my fingers loose, one by one, from a rusted muffin tin.

Of course, the drive to collect and retain isn't limited to older folks. And it isn't limited to humans. Animals hoard. But they mostly hoard food, and food is necessary for survival. Broken hair dryers aren't. It makes you wonder. What fears and insecurities are behind it all? Why do people assemble and refuse to relinquish things like a twenty-year collection of *National Geographic* magazines, stacked to the ceiling? To paraphrase Robert Frost, are they walling something in or walling something out?

And just try taking down the walls. You'll draw a sharp response: "That's *my* junk." We recognize this tendency in ourselves, but why are *things* so important to us?

And why, for instance, are clothes so important? Jesus told his disciples to "take nothing for their journey except a staff; no bread, no bag, no money in their belts; but to wear sandals and not to put on two tunics" (Mark 6:8-9). Jesus, of course, was a man, and he couldn't possibly appreciate the dilemma of a woman being restricted to even two tunics let alone one.

But I must admit that too much of a good thing is a burden. There are clothes in my closet that I'll never wear again. And they take up so much room. I have to wrestle with coat hangers in order to find a skirt I can actually wear. It's hard to breathe when things are so crowded. And breathing room is important, especially in the older years. We need space, open space: physically, mentally, spiritually.

Our lives are like a vineyard that has to be pruned so there'll be breathing room for grapes. When buds unfold in early spring, some of them have to be pinched off to provide open spaces. Then, in late summer, as the grapes start to change color, you have to thin out the canopy of foliage, exposing the clusters to light and air.

That's what I need to do. Prune, thin out, simplify the abundance of life. Reduce my wardrobe to one skirt and one sweater; sweep everything off the tables; sell the vases, dishes, glasses, pictures; give them away; pull down the curtains; and stand exposed and vulnerable before the Living God. With only a wooden bowl in my hands.

What would that be like? What was it like for St. Francis of Assisi to give away the sleeve of his robe with such careless abandon? I suppose if I were ever to do something like that, I'd respond the way my son did: "Now I've got room for lots more *things*." But, as with the game of garbage bags, that's not the point. *Emptiness* is the point. Not *things*.

And yet, when the shelves are empty, there *is* room for lots more. Not lots more *things*, but lots more Presence, as in the poetic reflection of R. S. Thomas called "The Absence:"

> It is this great absence
> that is like a presence, that compels
> me to address it without hope
> of a reply. It is a room I enter
>
> from which someone has just
> gone, the vestibule for the arrival
> of one who has not yet come.
> I modernize the anachronism
>
> of my language, but he is no more here
> than before. Genes and molecules
> have no more power to call
> him up than the incense of the Hebrews
>
> at their altars. My equations fail
> as my words do. What resource have I
> other than the emptiness without him of my whole
> being, a vacuum he may not abhor?[42]

The "emptiness without him" is like the emptiness that was in the beginning. The formless void was the "vestibule" for the arrival of the wind, the breath of God that swept over the face of the deep. It held such promise.

So, perhaps, when my own "equations fail," I should let go of a few more things. Useless things. And even a few treasures. Then, in the bounty of my emptiness, I can sing—ever so softly:

> Breathe on me Breath of God,
> fill me with life anew,
> that I may love what Thou dost love,
> and do what Thou woulds't do.[43]

Looking
Back

19

The Good Old Days

I REMEMBER the days when milk was delivered to your back door. In the winter it would freeze, and the paper cap would rise up out of the bottle on a column of cream. Those were the good old days. The days of soda fountains, rotary dials, juke boxes, and slow dancing to "Blue Moon" and "Stardust." Of the jitterbug—twirling in and out of your partner's arms to the rhythm of "Jack the Knife" and "Buttons and Bows." Of summer nights at the drive-in theater and *Movietone News* where you watched the boys raise a flag on Iwo Jima.

There were no seat belts in the cars, and to cool off you put your head out the open window and let the hot air rush across your face. There were no GameBoys or iPods for entertainment. But there were Burma Shave signs. "The chick he wed, let out a whoop; felt his chin, and flew the coop." The red and white flicker of those signs appeared every twenty-five miles along the highway.

Those were the good old days. Mostly. Sometimes the pleasure of memory is deceptive. Boredom in the backseat of the car was endless. "Stardust" was always the last dance, signaling an inevitable return to adolescent angst. And boys died on Iwo Jima. Mrs. Harrington's boy died. His name was Mike, and he used to let me drive his truck across the hills of Concan even though my feet could barely reach the floor. Mike smoked Lucky Strikes and blew smoke rings in a perfect O.

No, the way it "usta be" wasn't all that good. I saw the play *The Trip to Bountiful* recently, and in it the aging Carrie Watts remembers the good old days in Bountiful, her hometown near the Brazos River in Texas.

But cracks in her idealized memory appear in conversations. "I didn't use to worry. I was so carefree as a girl. Had lots to worry me, too. Everybody was so poor back in Bountiful. But we got along. I said to Papa once after our third crop failure in a row, whoever gave this place the name of Bountiful?"[44] "I used to work the land like a man. Had to when Papa died. . . . I got two little babies buried there. Renee Sue and Douglas. Diphtheria got Renee Sue. I never knew what carried Douglas away. He was just weak from the start."[45]

People say that memories of the "good old days" should include things like crop failures, Renee Sue, and Douglas. They lay all this stuff on us about being honest with ourselves. I say why? At our age we can afford the pleasure of self-deception. Carrie Watts was a prisoner of despair, shackled by city life. Her only space was a rocking chair where she sat, wrapped in her own arms, remembering the good old days in Bountiful. Memory, for all its idealization, gave her an escape. It gave form to a life that had become empty and meaningless.

But, once upon a time, life was beautiful, and sitting on the front gallery of her house, she could enjoy a soft breeze and the call of the whippoorwills. I say let the Carrie Watts of the world go home again. Let them indulge in deep nostalgia—scrape the cream off the top of the milk bottle and taste its sweetness. The skim will always be there, frozen beneath the surface.

And there's something really wonderful about deep nostalgia. It has an unbelievable power that won't allow the past to stay past. It pushes what-used-to-be up to the present and reshapes reality for the sake of well-being and new life. In Psalm 77, the speaker, much like Carrie Watts, lives in despair:

> In the day of my trouble I seek the Lord;
> in the night my hand is stretched out without wearying;
> my soul refuses to be comforted. (Psalm 77:2)

But even though he's so troubled he can't speak, the psalmist remembers the days of old.

> With your strong arm you redeemed your people,
> the descendents of Jacob and Joseph.
> When the waters saw you, O God, when the waters saw
>   you, they were afraid;
> the very deep trembled.
> The clouds poured out water;
> the skies thundered;
> your arrows flashed on every side. (Psalm 77:15-17)

Memories of the Exodus seem to rush into the present. They won't allow the psalmist to remain a prisoner of despair anymore than God allowed Israel to remain a prisoner of Egypt. Anymore than memories of Bountiful allow Carrie Watts to remain a prisoner of despair. Anymore than memories of the Last Supper allow us to remain prisoners of despair. "On the night before he was betrayed he took bread, said the blessing, broke the bread, and gave it to his friends, and said, 'Take, eat: This is my Body, which is given for you. Do this for the remembrance of me'" (Book of Common Prayer, 370-371).

And deep nostalgia seems to push itself not only into the present, but into the future. Carrie Watts, in the last scene of *The Trip to Bountiful,* stands on the rotting floorboards of her old house and says to her son, Ludie, "It's so quiet. It's so eternally quiet. I had forgotten the peace and the quiet. And it's given me strength once more, Ludie. To go on and do what I have to do. I've found my dignity and my strength."[46]

And what's most wonderful of all is that the life of Jesus pushes itself into the *future.* "Do not be alarmed; you are looking for Jesus of Nazareth, who was crucified. He has been raised; he is not here. . . . But go, tell his disciples and Peter that he is going ahead of you to Galilee; there you will see him"(Mark 16:6-7). The operative words are "ahead of you."

Those memories are all distant ones, but we old folks are really good at distant memories. Forget the short-term stuff.

"What's his name?" I can't remember, but I remember the good old days. I remember Burma Shave signs and smoke rings in a perfect O. I remember the shape of my first-born's skull in the cup of my hands and the smell of my husband's wool jacket, wet with rain.

I remember humankind being molded from the dust of the ground and the waters rolling back from the Red Sea; the taste of bread and wine in the company of friends; the empty tomb. Those memories give me dignity, and the strength to go on and do what I have to do.

20

A Mark of Grace

MRS. Lewis was our Sunday school teacher. She was an old woman, so thin you could sweep her away with the dust, but she was the best teacher in all of Christendom. She never made us memorize the commandments or recite the beatitudes or discuss the catechism. She told stories. Like the one in which the Lord God said to Jonah, "Go to Nineveh. Preach to them because they've been very bad." But Jonah—he didn't want to go to Nineveh. He didn't *know* anyone in Nineveh. So he boarded a ship that was going in the opposite direction. And no sooner was the ship under sail, than a huge storm came along—with waves as high as your chimney. The crew was scared to death and they decided that it was all Jonah's fault, because he had not done what the Lord told him to do. So they threw him overboard, into the middle of those huge waves. But Jonah—he was lucky. He ended up in the belly of a whale—just like Pinocchio—and the Lord God made the whale sneeze. Jonah flew out its mouth and onto a nice, warm, sandy beach. He picked himself up, brushed the sand off his legs, and said, "I guess I'd better go to Nineveh."

When Mrs. Lewis finished the story, we'd look at each other and sigh, as if we'd just finished a milk and cookie snack. And someone would usually stir long enough to say, "Tell it again, Mrs. Lewis."

Her stories invited us to step through the gates of imagination and identify with the characters—feel their sadness, fear, surprise, wonder, peace. And when we stepped back through the gates, we weren't the same. Somehow we stood a little taller, and bore a mark of grace on our foreheads. At least that's the way it always felt to me.

And as the years went by, I realized how Mrs. Lewis's bible stories provided a pattern for experiences that would otherwise have seemed to be mine alone. They gave me a language for expressing things that would otherwise have dissipated into a cloud of abstractions.

"I don't want to go to Nineveh."

But Mrs. Lewis has long since gone to her reward, so it's time for us to take her place in the circle. It's the function of elders to pass along the wisdom of their years. As Deuteronomy reminds us:

> Remember the days of old
> > consider the years long past;
> ask your father, and he will
> > inform you;
> your elders, and they will tell you. (Deuteronomy 32:7)

When the Hebrew fathers were asked to inform the young, they told stories about the years long past (with a few stretchers here and there). Stories about their ancestors—wandering Arameans—who planted their feet in the road and traveled the long journey of faith. Who went the wrong way sometimes and found themselves dumped on a nice, warm, sandy beach. Stories about God moving through the shadows, befriending those who were in alien lands, bending those who were rigid, healing those who were wounded.

In Chaim Potok's *Old Men at Midnight,* a character named Ilana Davita asks the old man if he had ever written down *his* stories. The old man says no.

"Then your stories will die with you," says Davita.

"So they will," says the old man. "Who needs stories of yet another Jew?"

"I need them," says Davita. "Without stories there is nothing. Stories are the world's memory. The past is erased without stories."[47]

We don't want the past to be erased, so we keep on talking. Hoping the next generation will find something of eternal significance in the delights and hazards we have experienced.

But it would be wrong for us to talk more than we listen. As William McNamara reminds his readers, "If I knew a renowned orator, an eloquent preacher, who talked all day long on the phone, on the job, on the street, and then jumped like a hot shot from a veritable Vesuvius of loquacity into the pulpit, I would not want to listen to him."[48]

My grandson never wanted to listen to "hot shots" either. When he was in his terrible two's (which extended over a period of eight years) he would cover up his ears if we said something he didn't want to hear, like "Stop picking up the cat by its neck." He refined his nonlistening skills with the addition of a *recitative fortissimo.*

"Lalalalalalalalala!"

But by the time we cross over the line into "older age," we've uncovered our ears and developed a taste for uncertainty that makes us more open to the truth of others. Like the apostles on the day of Pentecost when they all came together in one place. There was a miracle that day. And we usually think of it as a miracle of the tongue because they were telling stories in different languages. But, if you think about it, you begin to realize it wasn't a miracle of the tongue. It was a miracle of the ear. They uncovered their ears and *listened* to those who were speaking in different languages. That was the real miracle of it all.

And now that we've crossed over the line, we remember the days of old and consider the years long past with more understanding. We hear the story of a woman kneeling on cold stone all night, begging the angel of death to pass over, and we know the deeper layers of meaning in the story. We've been there. And we know how she felt when all she heard was the muffle of bats' wings. And then . . . how she lifted her head when the sun rose like a silk fan in the morning sky.

We hear the story of a man who was afraid he would be overwhelmed by it all, and then the waters parted, opened up in front of his eyes, and he was able to walk through on dry land. We've been there as well. And through stories like those we're more conscious of a pattern in experience that binds us all, one to the other, regardless of differences in culture, language, and religion. I guess that's what the Kingdom is all about.

"Without stories there is nothing."

I have lots of stories to tell. In fact, I could easily become a "veritable Vesuvius of loquacity." But I hope I can put a lid on it, because I think listening may be the last and best activity of life. And when we hear other stories, we'll somehow stand a little taller and bear a mark of grace on our foreheads. Perhaps we'll even stir long enough to say, "Tell it again. Please. Tell it again."

21

Out of the Whirlwind

WE usually think of wisdom as a good thing. It's certainly the last vestige of mental pride that we have when we're in the evening of life. We may not remember where we put our glasses, but we're wise. We're very, very wise. And it's important to share our wisdom—especially with those in the rush of youth.

So it was out of obligation that I decided to drive Kate back to college for her senior year. I should've let her go by herself (in the season of things, it was time) but letting go isn't easy. Besides, on the drive down there I could hold her captive in the front seat of the car for five hundred miles. And share my wisdom with her. Mile after mile of Mom's wisdom. About life and love and disappointment and failure and flossing teeth.

But I was only about an hour into sharing, when Kate turned to me and said, "Mom, what page are you on?"

In the silence of subsequent miles I remembered Job's rhetorical question: "Should the wise answer with windy knowledge?" (Job 15:2). I suppose one of the burdens of age is to separate wisdom from windy knowledge. Windy knowledge is grounded in past experience. It knows what it knows about the way things were and the way things ought to be. And it doesn't hesitate to offer its certainties for public consumption.

We probably get more windy as we get older. And that's understandable. Things change so fast, and our navigational systems are slow to adjust. They spin out of control when we see the curious world of modernity. Families have meals on the run between meetings and music lessons. They eat things like "chicken nuggets." Babies are never settled into play pens. Children are wired to "Game Boys." And no one writes letters. What's happened? Where are the headings that guided our course for so many years? As one grandfather observed, "When I was young I couldn't believe anything I read. Now I can't read anything I believe."

Change upsets our equilibrium. And on a level that's so primitive we can't fathom its depth, change is frightening. So we answer it with windy knowledge. Like Mary Magdalene that Easter morning when she rushes through the garden in protest: "They have taken away the body of my Lord." Past experience indicated that the reason for the empty tomb was robbery. What else could it have been? In the certainty of her knowledge, Mary Magdalene fails to see the risen Christ.

The eyes of Wisdom are open to new sources of truth. Walter Brueggemann, in a commentary on the practitioners of Wisdom in the Old Testament, said: "They are constantly facing new experience that must not only be integrated into the deposit of learning, but must be permitted to revise the deposit of learning in light of new data."[49] And when they revised those deposits of learning they could see that Yahweh was intimately involved in their day-to-day experience, and that the experience was "ordered, coherent, ethically reliable, and ethically insistent."[50]

That's not the way Job saw it. Job was blameless and upright in the eyes of the Lord, surrounded by friends, family, wealth, and honors. But suddenly his life turns to tragedy. All his children die in senseless accidents. His property is lost and his body is subjected to painful diseases. He can't understand. Why do such terrible things happen to good people? His friends answer with windy knowledge about the tradition of divine retribution: He must have done something terribly wrong.

But Job insists that he's done nothing:

If I have withheld anything that the poor desired,
or have caused the eyes of the widow to fail,
. . .
then let my shoulder blade fall from my shoulder,
and let my arm be broken from its socket. (Job 31:16-22)

Job can't understand why God doesn't fix things up. How can the Almighty be so distant and indifferent? Finally he hurls a challenge up to the throne of heaven. "Let the Almighty answer me!"

And the Almighty *does* answer him. After thirty-seven chapters of silence the Almighty speaks out of the whirlwind: "Who is this that darkens counsel by words without knowledge? Gird up your loins like a man, I will question you, and you shall declare to me" (Job 38:2-3). In other words, you may think that as the *image* of God, you are the *reality* of God. And that as the *reality* of God you can integrate new knowledge into your deposit of learning and see that life is "ordered, coherent, ethically reliable, and ethically insistent," but there's one problem—one big problem—your deposit of learning isn't as deep as you think it is. It's time for *you* to listen to *me*.

And then the Almighty instructs Job in the fundamentals of Wisdom:

> Where were you when I laid the foundation of the earth.
> Tell me, if you have understanding.
> Who determined its measurements—surely you know!
> or who stretched the line upon it?
> on what were its bases sunk,
> or who laid its cornerstone when the morning stars sang
>   together
> and all the heavenly beings shouted for joy? (Job 38:2-7)

Job doesn't speak. He just sits there—thinking. And finally he gets it. He understands: he isn't old enough to be wise! After all, he was only 120 years old. Much too young. In order to be wise and have the capacity to put all the pieces together, he had to have been there in the beginning when the Word was with God and the Word was God. Job wasn't there.

And neither was I. So there goes my last vestige of mental pride. Even if I learn to avoid windy knowledge; even if I integrate and revise new data; even if I eat "chicken nuggets," I'll never be wise enough to see that in spite of raging wars, abject poverty, and suffering innocence, life is "ordered, coherent, ethically reliable, and ethically insistent." I'm not old enough to see that.

But perhaps I'm old enough to earn a degree in *docta igno-rantia,* a learned ignorance. Those who earn such a degree "are not individuals who can tell you exactly who God is, where good and evil are and how to travel from this world to the next, but people whose articulate not-knowing makes them free to listen to the voice of God."[51]

And I'm sure that the voice of God will someday break through my shallow deposit of learning just the way it broke through Job's. Just the way it broke through Mary Magdalene's. "Indeed the word of God is living and active, sharper than any two-edged sword, piercing until it divides soul from spirit, joints from marrow" (Hebrews 4:12).

So perhaps one day I'll be able to tell my children what page I'm on. I'll be able to tell them I'm on the page that says even though the world appears more disordered than ordered, more incoherent than coherent, God is intimately involved in our day-to-day experience.

And, perhaps, by grace and a ragged, partial wisdom, I'll be able to stand with Job—in the face of windy knowledge—and proclaim with absolute certainty,

I know that my redeemer liveth,
and that he shall stand at the latter day upon the earth;
and though this body be destroyed, yet shall I see God;
whom I shall see for myself and mine eyes shall behold,
and not as a stranger. (Job 19:25-29)

22

Growing Old Together

Y OUNG people always think they invented sex. And that's wonderful. Their passion wouldn't be the same if they thought they were experiencing a hand-me-down or something their *parents* enjoyed. Engaged couples, obligated by church law to endure a certain amount of premarital counseling, used to sit in my office with their arms wrapped like kudzu vines around each other. Their smiles would be fixed and fearful. ("What if she talks to us about *sex*?") "Dear Lord," I'd pray, "you created them male and female. And you blessed them and told them to be fruitful and multiply. But did you *have* to make them so single-minded in that endeavor?"

Of course, you'd never want young couples to "love moderately" the way Friar Lawrence so foolishly advised Romeo and Juliet to love. As one Shakespeare critic observed, "Whoever heard of loving moderately?"[52] Counselors try to make the point that a young couple's immoderate love is a paradigm of God's love, but it's a message that's usually lost in the erotic steam that fills the office air.

At such times I'd often think about King David: "It happened, late one afternoon, when David rose from his couch and was walking about on the roof of the king's house, that he saw from the roof a woman bathing; the woman was very beautiful. David sent someone to inquire about the woman. It was reported, 'This is Bathsheba, daughter of Eliam, the wife of Uriah the Hittite." So

David sent messengers to get her, and she came to him and he lay with her" (2 Samuel 11:2-4).

There is, perhaps, no more tragic story of the tumultuous, consuming, possessive power of passion. It brings death to the husband who was betrayed, as well as to the child born of the illicit union. Wandering lust isn't usually an immediate issue with young lovers—they're too exclusive—but the power of passion to make us blind to reason and right order is an issue. That's why, when as families and friends, we gather to witness wedding vows, we need to pray that the young man and woman standing at the altar, making all those unrealistic promises, will survive the early stages of their relationship.

The late Rev. Thom Blair, in an article entitled "In Praise of Old Age and Aged Marriages" offered this advice on marriage:

> The only way to avoid very serious marital troubles is not to get married. My encouraging word is that the first fifty years are the hardest. After that it gets easy. I submit that this is so because those early years are spent working through the impossibilities of this thing called marriage. . . . As the years go by, you might decide you are too tired to keep up the struggle to be the one in charge. You decide that it is easier to muddle through, being thankful when you get your way, but knowing it won't last long. . . . As the years go by, you might give up your hope of reforming the other. . . . As the years go by, time or medicine or surgeons may well have done sex in. That is bad. But if you can find some way to live without sex, life starts to get simpler. . . . As the years go by, you have been through better and worse, sickness and health, richer and poorer, hell and high water. What binds you together is deeper and broader and higher than you ever imagined was possible. Now you can begin to know what love is.[53]

It's an incomparable blessing to have a companion with whom you can work through "the impossibilities of this thing called marriage," and work through them successfully (success being a relative measure). It's what prompted Tobit to pray on the night he was wed to Sarah, "Grant that she and I may find mercy and that we may grow old together. And they both said, 'Amen, Amen.'" (Tobit 8:7-8).

Even in God's mercy, married couples will usually face a crisis that shakes the very foundation of their lives. If the foundation holds, and the residue of inarticulate grief draws them into deeper communion with the suffering Christ, they can begin to know what love is.

And, hopefully, that love will acquire what C. S. Lewis calls the "homespun clothing of affection."[54] Affection is a love that is wrapped around us as the years go by, after we have survived many crises together. It's a love that's not so insistent on self-gratification. Rather, it thrives on the simple comfort of another's presence. Conversations have the ease of unguarded moments. Silence can be eloquent. And the familiar warmth of the one beside you, wearing the same old, worn pajamas, can awaken a heart of deep tenderness.

Wallace Stegner, at the end of his novel *The Spectator Bird*, says of this love in later life:

> The truest vision of life I know is that bird in the Venerable Bede that flutters from the dark into a lighted hall, and after a while flutters out again into the dark. . . . It is something— it can be everything—to have found a fellow bird with whom you can sit among the rafters while the drinking and boasting and reciting and fighting go on below; a fellow bird whom you can look after and find bugs and seeds for; one who will patch your bruises and straighten your ruffled feathers and mourn over your hurts when you accidentally fly into something you can't handle.[55]

I suppose the thing you fly into that's the most difficult to handle is your mutual mortality. You won't be able to exit life the way you exit the movie theater, holding hands and wondering where you parked the car.

Mythology is steeped in the pain of this anticipated separation. When Philemon and Baucis, both full of years, entertain Zeus and Hermes, the gods decide to reward the couple for their hospitality. "Tell us what you would like as a reward," they say.

The old couple confers and finally makes a request. "Let us die together so that we never have to see the other's tomb."

Unfortunately, that request is rarely granted. The partner left behind must tend the other's grave, and look to the place nearby where someday he or she will lie in rest. And yet old lovers leave a legacy for the young because what binds them together, even when separated by death, is deeper and broader and higher than they ever imagined was possible. In Wendell Berry's poem "To Tanya at Christmas," the poet speaks to this legacy:

> our lives rise
> in speech to our children's tongues.
> They will tell how we once stood
> together here, two trees
> whose lives in annual sheddings
> made their way into this ground,
> whose bodies turned to earth
> and song. The song will tell
> how old love sweetens the fields.[56]

Amen. Amen.

Under
the
Shadows

23

Sunshine Havens

I T was too late to transplant the irises. I knew that, but I tried it anyway. The plants survived the shock, but they didn't bloom. On the other hand, we once transplanted a magnolia tree that everyone said would never survive, because it faced the north wind. But it's standing tall now. The leaves are glossy green, and in the spring it produces creamy blossoms so sweet they fill the house with their fragrance.

I guess the success of transplanting depends on the age and the tenacity of the plant. The same is true with older folks. At some point in our later years, diminishing strength and health dictate a change in living arrangements—a move to an apartment, a retirement community, a long-term care facility. For some it's an easy decision. They recognize the necessity and they plan ahead. But for others, it's not so easy. They're convinced they're too old to be transplanted. Families have to force the decision. They gather around the old dining room table and talk:

"Mom could fall and no one would be here to help her."

"And she's so forgetful. I was here yesterday and her Thursday meds were still sitting on the counter."

"She needs to sell this place."

"Then what? Where does she go? I mean, none of us can take care of her."

"I have a guest room, but she'd have to share a bath with the kids and the kids would drive her crazy. Besides, she'd be alone in the house all day"

"What about Homestead Manor?"

"Too expensive."

"There's that place out at North St. called Sunshine Haven, or something like that. They say it's reasonable. She could even have a private room."

And so it goes. Around and around. Meanwhile, the prospective "transplantee" feels manipulated. "They keep referring to me as 'she.' Like I was someone they didn't know. And if they think I'm leaving this place, they've got another think coming."

I'll probably feel the same way when my time comes.

But everyone gets real excited about Sunshine Haven, "where happiness consists in small conveniences that occur every day." "It's so nice, Mama. You'll love it." Mama looks at the apartment with its two-toned carpet and Pullman kitchen, and decides that "small conveniences" aren't worth it. The family forces the decision.

"Very truly, I tell you, when you were younger, you used to fasten your own belt and to go wherever you wished. But when you grow old, you will stretch out your hands, and someone else will fasten a belt around you and take you where you do not wish to go" (John 21:18).

Mama moves to Sunshine Haven. The dresser doesn't fit where she thought it would, and never mind the recliner. It won't make it through the door. The ice box only has two shelves. Outside the window, beyond the air conditioner units, she can see the mountains where home is bunkered up against the hillside.

Home was spacious. On holidays there'd be fifteen people sitting around the table. There was a swing on the back porch and it squeaked with every to and fro. Her son put some WD40—or was it 24D—she forgets which is which—but he put some on the swing thinking he could fix the squeak. Praise the Lord, it didn't work.

She and Papa slept in the front bedroom. They whispered so the children wouldn't hear. The walls were papered in patterns of lilac blooms and a few water stains that blended with the tangled leaves.

Home.

It was beautiful.

I certainly don't want to leave my home. Some elders never survive the move. Others survive but they never bloom again, mostly because they shrivel up in in self-pity. And yet I know so many who, like transplanted irises, do settle their roots deep into the new soil. They not only survive; they bloom again.

Which is not to say they're without suffering. It's just that their suffering has a voice like that of the psalmist who speaks for the Jews who were exiled to Babylon, away from home, away from Jerusalem:

> By the rivers of Babylon—
> there we sat down and there we wept
> when we remembered Zion.
> On the willows there we hung up our harps.
> For there our captors asked us for songs,
> and our tormentors asked for mirth, saying
> Sing us one of the songs of Zion. (Psalm 137:1-3)

The psalmist's deep longing for home is compounded by the offense of captors who require the exiles to sing sacred songs for public amusement. But what's amazing is that even in the face of humiliation, the exiles cling to a vision of their homecoming:

> So the ransomed of the Lord shall return,
> and come to Zion with singing;
> everlasting joy shall be upon their heads;
> they shall obtain joy and gladness,
> and sorrow and sighing shall flee away. (Isaiah 35:10)

I know many older folks in Sunshine Havens who not only look to the future with the hope of everlasting joy, but they also live in the moment with a grateful gladness. Because, aside from providing "small conveniences that occur every day," their Sunshine Haven provides a community. It makes them feel they belong. That they're not alone. And for me, having a sense of community seems more and more important with every step along the way.

But the residents of Sunshine Havens share something that we'll never have until we settle down in their soil. And that's a bond that develops out of the deep knowledge of human mortality. Because of that deep knowledge, they need each other, just the way the exiled Jews needed each other, in order to sustain a vision of the ransomed of the Lord returning home. Together they can face the north wind with tenacity. And everlasting joy shall be upon their heads.

24

God's Spies

THOSE of us on the other side of seventy grew up in a culture in which freedom was limited. There was a consortium of power that ruled over us. And in a conflict, no matter what we did, our parents agreed with the consortium—which included teachers, principals, clergy, neighbors, librarians, "and practically anybody else older or taller than we were," as author Peter Gomes recalls.[57] It was usually a benevolent tyranny, but I frequently had to "serve time" for things done and left undone. When I was fifteen years old, my parents decided that I would be better off where there was "more structure," so they sent me away to a religious boarding school. Fortunately, my sister went with me, and we were able to enter the hallowed gates together.

There were a lot of dos and don'ts and oughts and shoulds at that school. No one ever mentioned "individual rights" or "entitlements." We more or less had to make a Pauline choice between being a slave to Christ or a slave to sin. We studied, played vigorous sports (lest we think about the pleasures that those outside our walls enjoyed), and went to chapel every day—kneeling on Spanish tiles until our legs were numb. Friday afternoons we were allowed to walk to town in two straight lines, escorted by a chaperone who saw to it that we didn't buy any contraband. Contraband, in those days, consisted of lipstick, chewing gum, and movie magazines.

On Sundays we enjoyed a little freedom. Instead of going to study hall, we were invited to sit in the drawing room and listen to Miss Cummins read *The Odyssey*. Miss Cummins was the headmistress. She was stately, tall, and strict. But on Sunday afternoons she seemed to forget that she was headmistress. Or maybe we forgot. She would get all caught up in the story of brave Telemachus. Her eyes would sparkle and her cheeks would get all rosy, like she was human or something.

When I tell young people about my boarding school days, they find it hard to believe. Surely, they say, I am lifting scenes out of a nineteenth-century novel. But as Peter Gomes said in *The Good Life,* "I lived in such a place . . . and in an environment that to some, perhaps then and certainly now, might seem stifling, uncreative, and even repressed, I felt free to grow."[58]

Then, when I was finally an adult, came the sixties and seventies—an era that roared into history with a wave of protest against consortiums of power. Colonies in Africa hauled down the Union Jack and raised the flags of indigenous people; the American civil rights movement caught fire with the clarion call of Martin Luther King Jr.; women locked arms and dared to stand together in the face of ancient barriers; rebellions on college campuses offered a new license for living. As Peter Gomes describes it, "Freedom now became the warrant for self-expression, self-determination, and the ticket to what would be the new good life. In place of deference, authority, and community there arose a new ideology of the self: individualism."[59] We were swept away in the spirit of the age, one reminiscent of the scriptural claim, "For freedom Christ has set us free. Stand firm, therefore, and do not submit to a yoke of slavery" (Galatians 5:1).

Then came the eighties, nineties, and finally the turn of the millennium. We were older. But having enjoyed the sweet taste of freedom, we entered our older years with a determination to stand firm and assert our right to self-expression—with the bravado and chutzpah described by the poet, Jenny Joseph, who claimed "When I am an old woman, I shall wear purple / . . . And run my stick along the public railings / And make up for the sobriety of my youth."[60] Joseph's plan sounds like a good one, although I suppose we'll eventually run out of bravado. The limits of health, energy, mobility, and memory will rein in our freedom, reversing decades of cherished independence.

Our children will decide we'd be better off where there is "more structure." They'll move us into supervised housing where we'll greet each other as fellow "inmates." Administrators, nurses, dieticians, security guards, and housekeepers will stand in loco parentis. Then one day the consortium of power will decide it's dangerous for us to drive down the highway with our left turn signals blinking. And in a coup e'etat, they'll take away our car keys! The warrant for self-determination will be torn in two.

Helen M. Luke, in her book called *Old Age: A Journey into Simplicity* cites King Lear's address to the faithful daughter, Cordelia, at the end of the play. Cordelia, in the passion of her youth, wants to lock arms and go out to meet the enemy, but Lear refuses:

> No, no, no! Come, let's away to prison:
> We two alone will sing like birds i' the cage;
> When thou dost ask me blessing, I'll kneel down
> And ask of thee forgiveness: so we'll live,
> And pray and sing, and tell old tales, and laugh
> At gilded butterflies, and hear poor rogues
> Talk of court news; and we'll talk with them too, —
> Who loses and who wins; who's in, and who's out: —
> And take upon's the mystery of things,
> As if we were God's spies: and we'll wear out,
> In a wall'd prison, packs and sects of great ones,
> That ebb and flow by th' moon.
> (William Shakespeare, *King Lear*, Act 5, Scene 3, lines 8-19)

Ironically, the surrender to a walled prison is a liberation for the aging, disillusioned Lear. He imagines the reciprocal relationship of father and daughter—kneeling, blessing, forgiving—without regard for hierarchy; telling old tales without regard for the fanatical disputes of political parties; and taking upon himself the "mystery of things." He doesn't want to *solve* the mystery; he doesn't even want to *understand* it. He just wants to enter it.

Like those of our generation who, in our childhoods, lived in a culture of deference, authority, and community, Lear seems to understand that as Gomes says, in "an environment that might . . . seem stifling, uncreative, and even repressed," he'd be free to grow.

I'm not *quite* ready to be free to grow. I need a few more years to make up for the sobriety of my youth. Before I hand over the keys, I'd like to drive to the edge of the ocean and back again—in a convertible; cruise down the Amalfi coast—listening to Verdi's *Un Di Felice;* I'd like to climb the Rising Sun Highway in Montana. Then, when I come home, I'd like to pile the grandchildren into the back of the station wagon, let them roll around like tennis balls, and drive down to the lake—listening to James Taylor's *How Sweet It Is to be Loved by You.* Then maybe I'll be ready to respond to the invitation to come away to prison. I'll give up my car keys and settle down to singing, praying, laughing, telling old tales—about boarding schools and gilded butterflies. Letting the chains of self-determination fall at my feet. Maybe I'll even be one of God's spies.

25

Necessary Resistance

A S I move into old age, I realize how much the English language has changed in my lifetime. There was a time when a "significant relationship" meant being able to sit down and talk to your teacher, and "pot" was something your mother used when she boiled potatoes. Language changes, evolves, takes on new meaning. That's probably why there's a lot of confusion about the words, *acceptance* and *submission* these days.

Acceptance is sort of like riding ocean waves. I can't ride them anymore, but I remember how you had to float on the swells, then paddle quickly to the crests, and let the spills carry you, laughing, all the way to shore. It was fun. And it evoked a feeling of strength and cooperation with the deep rhythm of the tide. Acceptance evokes a similar feeling. Like the crest of a wave, the Annunciation came in the fullness of time. And when Mary said "Let it be according to thy word," she must have felt empowered by a deep rhythm.

Submission is another thing altogether. Submission weakens people. In its modern context, it has negative connotations of domination, arbitrary commands and a great distance separating the commander and the commandee. There was no distance between Mary and Gabriel, and none between Gabriel and God.

A lot of people think that when we enter the final stage of life, we become—or should become—more submissive. I don't agree. I think we need to learn the art of acceptance—about limits and such—and live in the rhythm of our days, but we certainly aren't supposed to wilt like yesterday's flowers. After all, the bible glorifies those who are full of days, because of their strength, not because of their weakness. Caleb, having received Hebron in the division of Canaan, brags, "See, I am here today, eighty-five years old. I am still as strong as the day Moses sent me out; I am just as vigorous to go out to battle now as I was then" (Joshua 14:10-11). Sometimes we need to go out to battle even if all we can do is raise an aging voice in protest.

My mother was particularly good at raising her aging voice in protest. She protested, among other things, Prohibition, the New Deal, Yankees, long skirts, short skirts, microwaves, motor boats, the new prayer book, and children with runny noses. Her vigorous spirit hardened as she moved deeper into the final stage of life, causing problems for the caretakers at her nursing home.

One day the supervisor called and asked me to come down so we could talk. I had received similar telephone calls from the children's school principals, and the invitation to talk usually meant trouble. So I went to see the supervisor with an uneasy feeling.

The feeling was justified. Apparently my mother had decided to put her left shoe on her right foot, and her right shoe on her left foot. The nurses, who were very concerned about anything that might make walking hazardous, had tried to exchange the shoes. But my mother yelled in protest. Then, surprised at the power of her own voice, she yelled again. It worked. The sea of white uniforms parted and my mother clomped her way down the corridor—left foot, right foot, clomp, clomp, clomp.

Unfortunately, the taste of victory was so sweet that she started exercising the yell more often. She yelled when it was time to take a bath. She yelled when someone changed the television channel. The nurses called her behavior "oppositional." I agreed, and suggested that if they ignored her for a while, she might quit. But I really hoped they would let her have her way when it came to things like shoes.

Somehow it seemed to me that, however oppositional my mother's behavior might have been, it was a necessary resistance, to protest the total loss of self-determination. Those who "knew better" usually made decisions for her. "Sign here," they said, and so she would. But those who "knew better" did not know my mother. She was no reed shaken by the wind. She clung to whatever authority she had left, even if the only decision she could make was what shoe to put on what foot.

It's been years now since my mother won that skirmish in the nursing corridor. As time went by, she resorted to other forms of rebellion like smoking cigarettes and wearing two dresses, one on top of the other. One morning she packed her suitcase and said she was going to Paris. But slowly she began to relax her iron fist, spending more time in bed, watching clouds gather in the mottled sky. Then one August afternoon, when the sun hung hot against the hillsides, she crumpled her last protest, and let go completely.

Her leaving left a great stillness in the air.

Now that I'm a little older, I've gained more respect for my mother's oppositional behavior. And I'm still willing and able to protest when it comes to issues of discrimination, neglect, and unnecessary losses.

A friend of mine recently protested a change in zoning because, while the developers were building less expensive houses, (and she agreed that such houses were needed) they were all two-story houses. Whoever heard of older folk being able to go up and down stairs all day, especially if their shoes are on the wrong feet?

Some things deserve a good yell.

26

Sharing the Same Sidewalks

OUR mission in New York was a serious one. We were looking for a "Walkman," that portable music box that was the new toy of the eighties. My daughters assured me that I needed one as much as they did, so we shopped at every store on 46th Street, to compare the prices. Finally, Kate announced at Sounds Alive, "We'll take three of them," as if she were ordering salted pretzels from a vendor's cart.

Sally showed me how to fix the shoulder strap and adjust the earphones to my head. And then, at the touch of a metal button, I opened my own concert hall—with the sound of flutes and violins in stereo. The girls opened their concert hall with the sound of drums and steel guitars.

We walked to separate rhythms that day, but stayed close to each other so we could admire the knitted vests and linen skirts in windows along the way. It was June again, with its season of laughter in full bloom. And although we circumscribed ourselves with private sounds, we shared the same sidewalk.

A few years later the girls graduated from high school. They went off to college, married, and had children of their own. Our sidewalks separated, leaving me with a deep nostalgia, especially when it was June again.

There was a time—long ago—when families didn't separate. They lived together in one place. The earth settled beneath their feet. Generations of cousins, uncles, aunts, and sundry in-laws supported each other, and children not only showed parents how to fix shoulder straps, but they also took full responsibility for them in their old age.

In the book of Tobit, the father in his old age reminds his son to "honor" his mother. And in those days "honor" meant a lot more than courteous respect. "Do not abandon her all the days of her life. Do whatever pleases her, and do not grieve her in anything. Remember her, my son because she faced many dangers for you while you were in her womb. And when she dies, bury her beside me in the same grave" (Sirach 3:12-13).

Things have changed since biblical days. We're far more self-sufficient. Instead of depending on sons and daughters for support, many of us enjoy pensions, Social Security, and medical benefits. We drive south to get warm in the winter and north to get cool in the summer. Meanwhile, our children move away to places like Milwaukee and San Bernadino. They honor us by email.

And we have no choice but to accept the situation. Mobility is part of modern culture. And it does have some benefits. As Kahlil Gibran advises: "Let there be spaces in your togetherness, And let the winds of the heavens dance between you."[61] It's always nice to welcome the winds of heaven. Especially after children and grandchildren have come home for Christmas. There are very few spaces in the togetherness of Christmas. And there's lots to do. You deck the halls, wrap presents, make beds, cook turkeys, wash dishes, feed babies, play games, greet friends, perk coffee, burn candles, fill stockings, mend toys, wash dishes, settle fights, sweep floors, and adore Jesus.

But soon it's time for the children to go. The car doors are locked and they drive away in a sweet cloud of dust. I remember one time when they turned around and came back. It was a shocking experience. They had forgotten a jacket or something, but for an instant I was actually scared.

Then it was June again. And I tried to remember the details of that day in New York twenty years ago—what the girls wore, how they fixed their hair. I think we bought some chocolate truffles on our way back to Grand Central.

There's always a hint of loneliness in the air when children are gone.

But it makes me wonder if the loneliness can be consecrated—turned into something holy. Henri Nouwen, in his book *Reaching Out,* says we need to convert our loneliness to solitude: "Instead of running away from our loneliness and trying to forget or deny it, we have to protect it and turn it into a fruitful solitude. To live a spiritual life we must first find the courage to enter into the desert of our loneliness and to change it by gentle and persistent efforts into a garden of solitude."[62]

It seems strange to talk about "protecting" our loneliness, as if it were a treasure or something. But the more you think about it, the more obvious it is that without the experience of loneliness, we wouldn't have a desire to fill the void. We wouldn't feel the thirst of the desert.

So, ironically, loneliness can become something positive, a force that leads us into what we desire most—fulfillment.

And, according to the mystics, true fulfillment can be found only in a garden of solitude. A place where, in the ultimate depths of each individual soul, we can meet God. And where we can hear the voice of God, the way Elijah did, in the sound of sheer silence.

Thomas Merton, who lived the last years of his life as a hermit, lovingly describes his place of solitude:

> [A] fine place to read and pray, on the top floor of that barn building where the rabbits used to be. Up under the roof is a place reached by various ladders. Some stovepipes and old buckets are there and many little boxes in which the novices gather strawberries in the early summertime. There is a chair and there is a beautiful small rectangular window which faces south over the valley—the further orchard, Saint Joseph's field, the distant line of hills.[63]

It's not always necessary to climb up under the roof between stovepipes and buckets to find solitude. Some people can find it in a flock of people, walking from room to room in a crowded museum, or riding a commuter train through the boroughs at rush hour. They have an amazing capacity to block out the prattle and enter their own sanctuary.

But the truth is that a sanctuary is actually full of people, even when it's on the top floor of a barn where the rabbits used to be. There's really no such thing as "privacy" in solitude, because we have generations of friends and neighbors and brothers and sisters and cousins and in-laws with us—united through Christ, one to the other. And the bond is so tight—even with those who are strangers—that we can't let go of them even when we climb up various ladders to find our solitude. So how can we be lonely?

We all walk to separate rhythms and the winds of heaven are dancing between us, but I like to think that we're sharing the same sidewalk. We stay close to each other. And sometimes, even when it's wintertime and the sky is heavy on the distant line of hills, it seems as if it's June again. And the season of laughter is in full bloom.

The
Last
Few
Miles

27

A Dignified Dependence

HIKING the Appalachian Trail early one spring, I encountered a swollen creek, which was not unusual at that time of the year. To get to the other side, you had to step from one rock to another, balancing on the flattest surface you could find. It's always a hazardous crossing, and when you're carrying twenty-five pounds on your back, the slightest misstep can cause the weight to shift perilously to one side. I misstepped. The weight shifted, and I fell backwards into the creek.

Fortunately, my pack cushioned the fall, but as water poured through the pockets, sleeping bag, wool sweater, and flannel pajamas, it became impossible for me to right myself. I was as helpless as a turtle on its back, arms and legs flailing the air. And, to make matters worse, my children thought I looked funny. They denied it, of course. "I didn't laugh, Mom. I promise. I was just coughing." But I saw them. They laughed. Then, feeling filial shame, they pulled me to my feet and helped me slosh up the hillside in wet socks.

The "turtling" accident occurred a long time ago, yet I still remember it, especially when I try to do something awkward—like climbing out of the bathtub. I feel so helpless. And I'm sure I look funny. But as the years go by, the trend isn't going to reverse itself. I'm not likely to wake up one morning full of grace.

Of course, I'll continue getting those routine medical exams—waiting a long time in the reception room, then waiting a long time in the doctor-will-be-here-in-just-a-moment room—looking at walls covered with illustrations of the human anatomy—knee bones connected to thigh bones—and digestive tracks indecently exposed to the public eye.

But, in spite of all the medical oversight, I know that at some point down the road I'll become truly helpless and totally dependent on others to pull me to my feet. That's what happens when you live to a ripe old age. A back that was once tall and straight becomes bent with arthritic age. Bones break. They take months to heal, if they heal at all. Arms are suddenly paralyzed and hang by the side like useless rags. Speech is impaired, and no matter how much you try to explain something, no one understands. Oxygen is scarce. Cancer cells march through the body with devastating impact.

Donald X. Burt describes the body's decline:

> The great athlete may in the end find it difficult to walk. The great manager may eventually find it impossible to manage even his own body functions. The great thinker may come to spend more time in forgetting than in knowing—sometime standing perplexed in the middle of the room confused about where to go. . . . The great saviors who spent their lifetime carrying the weak and wounded on their backs, may come to depend entirely on others—others who must be *paid* to feed them and clean them and sit them by a window for a breath of air.[64]

People seem to accept the condition of helplessness in the same way they accepted adversity in their youth. Those who wallowed in self-pity when they were young will wallow when they're old. Those who accepted adversity with resilient grace when they were young, will accept it with resilient grace when they're old.

I'll probably wallow—at least a little bit.

But I hope I'll also be one of those who pray, perhaps using one of my favorites from the Book of Common Prayer:

> This is another day, O Lord. I know not what it will bring forth, but make me ready, Lord, for whatever it may be. If I

am to stand up, help me to stand bravely. If I am to sit still, help me to sit quietly. If I am to lie low, help me to do it patiently. And if I am to do nothing, let me do it gallantly. Make these more than words, and give me the Spirit of Jesus. (Book of Common Prayer, 461)

While I don't like the prospect of doing nothing gallantly, it's sometimes necessary. St. Augustine draws an analogy to a herd of deer crossing a dangerous stretch of water:

> They organize themselves in a single line so that, as they swim, the heavy weight of their antlered head can be supported by the flank of the deer ahead. The buck at the front has no support but after a time he will yield his place to the second in line and himself go to the rear where he may take some rest. In this way the entire group of deer, by bearing one another's burden, are able to cross even the most difficult channel to solid ground.[65]

We have to swallow a lot of pride when we yield our place in line. But if we yield with gratitude instead of tiresome apologies and self-deprecations, we'll achieve something extraordinary in our later years. We'll give others the opportunity to love us even though we're useless, crippled, blind, deaf, and incontinent. Even though we're not naturally lovable.

Of course, we want people to love us because we *are* lovable; because we're attractive, strong, successful; because we're well-coifed, well-dressed, well-trimmed. But that's not the case when we're lying on our backs in a creek bed with arms and legs flailing the air. We're laughable, not lovable. But in the ironic mystery of God, we're also instruments of a graceless grace. We're planting seeds for others to grow in what the old bible called "charity."

In Paul's language the word *charity* has nothing to do with the modern condescension of tasteful donations. It has to do with a form of love that isn't hungry or needy or longing to be filled. It has to do with a form of love that wants—above all else—to offer care and tenderness and blessings to the beloved until his eyes are brimming over with gladness. That kind of love is totally gratuitous. "It bears all things, believes all things, hopes all things, endures all things" (1 Corinthians 13:7). And if we can let others "practice" that kind love on us, think of what the world might be like someday! No more noisy gongs or clanging cymbals. And we'll be heroes—all of us—toothless, deaf, upended heroes!

And when the end comes, and someone pulls me up and sets my wet feet on firmer ground, I hope I'll say "thank you," and I hope I'll remember to proclaim for all the earthly elders to hear, "Sometimes it is more blessed to receive than to give."

28

Chasing a Star

IN my older age I've developed a fascination for angels. Not the dimpled cherubs of Western paintings and Victorian memorabilia, but "real" angels, like those in the books of Daniel and Revelation: "I looked up and saw a man clothed in linen, with a belt of gold from Uphaz around his waist. His body was like beryl, his face like lightning, his eyes like flaming torches, his arms and legs like the gleam of burnished bronze, and the sound of his words like the roar of a multitude" (Daniel 10:5-6). That's a *real* angel. A holy warrior.

Angels are more mysterious when they appear in Jacob's dream at Bethel. Of course, Jacob is very anxious at the time, having cheated his brother out of birthright and blessing. Leaving Beer-Sheba on the run, he heads for Haran, and at the end of the first day, he finds a level place on the hillside where he can tether his camel and stay for the night. Looking up at the sky with its canopy of light, he falls asleep and breathes the deep rhythm of time. Then the dream begins. There's a ladder with a thousand rungs reaching all the way to heaven. And ascending and descending the ladder are a myriad of angels with wings the length of eagles' wings. Their movement sounds like the rush of wind on the desert sand. Their feet never touch the ground. Jacob believes the place is none other than the gate of heaven.

It's a scene that stirs the imagination, but the meaning and authority of those angels varies with every age and every interpretation. During the Reformation Calvin took a minimalist approach, but in *Paradise Lost* Milton presented angels as radically free demigods. Then with the Enlightenment—when everyone was so terribly reasonable—science dismissed all celestial creatures as part of an antique worldview.

Today, however, angels are enjoying a popular revival. They're tracked on the "Angel Watch Network." They have even had their own prime-time television show. And parallel to their New Age publicity is a fascination, like mine, with the Orthodox perspective. In the East, angels are understood to be pure spirits—created to worship and reflect divine beauty, and to do the will of God wherever God sends them.

I've painted two biblical angels—Michael and Gabriel—in iconography classes. Their hands are smudged and their eyes are a bit off-center, but I think of these angels as companions on the way. What's amazing, however, is that the carefully-ordered process of "writing" an icon—beginning with clay and continuing through dark pigments and floats that ascend into bright colors— is intended to be a spiritual exercise. In other words, as the image of the angel emerges in the icon, it's also supposed to emerge in me! Like the archangels Michael and Gabriel, I'm meant to worship and reflect divine beauty and do the will of God wherever God sends me. That's a real stretch. But the whole process is based on the belief that God became human in order that we might become divine.

The idea of divinization has received only a passing nod in the West, probably because we're too hooked on original sin to acknowledge the possibility. But according to Orthodox Christianity, there's a development of the person from baptism to old age in which we're called not simply to accept forensic justification, but to change, mature, grow, and be transfigured into the image of the divine.

I don't think there's any possibility of my changing, maturing, growing, and being transfigured into an angel, especially if it means having a body like beryl, a face like lightning, and eyes like flaming torches. And it always makes me anxious when I hear Jesus say, "Be perfect, therefore, as your heavenly Father is perfect" (Matthew 5:48). Perfection, like divinity, seems impossible.

Gregory of Nyssa acknowledged this anxiety:

Though it may not be possible completely to attain the ultimate and sovereign good, it is most desirable for those who
are wise to have at least a share in it. We should then make
every effort not to fall short utterly of the perfection that is
possible for us, and try to come as close to it and possess as
much of it as possible.[66]

There's the challenge. And quite a challenge it is for those of
us in our later years. We're so settled in our ways, and even
though we may sometimes be wrong, we're never in doubt. And
as far as "spiritual development" is concerned, we're happy to sit
in a rickshaw, read the *New York Times*, and let Grace pull us
around town. So sharing in the sovereign good might be difficult.

But with my companions on the way, I hope I can at least try.
There's something to be said for the effort, for the *desire* to be
attentive to covenant, the *desire* to imitate the angels in the asceti-
cal life of prayer, the *desire* to be messengers, guardians, light bear-
ers, holy warriors. There's something to be said for a soul that
longs, like a deer for the water-brooks, for the living God.

It's easy to dismiss all the effort with the excuse that we're too
old. I use that excuse whenever I need it. But then I think about
the angels. They're more ancient than the stars.

And I think about the moth in James Thurber's fable. He was
a young and impressionable moth with the desire to reach for the
impossible.

[He]set his heart on a certain star. He told his mother about
this and she counseled him to set his heart on a bridge lamp
instead. "Stars aren't the thing to hang around," she said;
"lamps are the thing to hang around." "You get somewhere
that way," said the moth's father. "You don't get anywhere
chasing stars. But the moth would not heed the words of
either parent. Every evening at dusk when the star came
out he would start flying toward it and every morning at
dawn he would crawl back home worn out with his vain
endeavor. One day his father said to him, "You haven't
burned a wing in months, boy, and it looks to me as if you
were never going to. All your brothers have been badly

burned flying around street lamps and all your sisters have been terribly singed flying around house lamps. Come on, now, get out of here and get yourself scorched! A big strapping moth like you without a mark on him!"

The moth left his father's house, but he would not fly around street lamps and he would not fly around house lamps. He went right on trying to reach the star, which was four and one-third light years, or twenty-five trillion miles, away. The moth thought it was just caught in the top branches of an elm. He never did reach the star, but he went right on trying, night after night, and when he was a very, very old moth he began to think that he really had reached the star. . . . This gave him a deep and lasting pleasure, and he lived to a great old age.[67]

So I'm going to keep my sights on the star that is four and one-third light years away. Recognizing the value of the effort. And as the years go by, I'm going to depend more and more on my companions, Michael and Gabriel. When I get so arthritic that my moth-like wings won't even flutter, I hope to see them ascending and descending the ladder with a thousand rungs. And as I reach up for a share of the sovereign good, I hope they'll reach down and pull me up—past bridge lamps and street lamps, through moons and silver night until we reach the gates of heaven. Who knows—my feet may never again touch the ground.

29

A Dozen Eggs

MY mother lived the last fifteen years of her life in a retirement home. She complained, of course, about the rules, and the people who talked too much, and the overcooked broccoli, but she was moderately content with her residence.

One evening, when I was having a quiet meal with her in the dining hall, she turned to me and said, "Jane, I really like saying that confession—you know—about all my manifold sins and wickedness, but tell me, Jane," and she moved in a little closer, "what *are* my sins?" With that she swept her hand across a sea of white-headed women, and said, "How can anyone *sin* in a place like this?"

Well, I backed off that one real fast. But like many in her generation, my mother identified sin with sex. And the deterrent to sin was fear that one might end up like Hester Prynne in *The Scarlet Letter,* standing on the scaffold of the pillory with the weight of a thousand eyes fastened on her mark of shame.

Fortunately, the meaning of sin has expanded slightly in recent decades to include the deep injustices of a life lived in violation of covenant and communion.

But now that I'm a lot older, my mother's question has a certain "end of life" urgency. I don't want to "die unprepared." And having more time to remember, I can begin to gather up my own "manifold sins." It's like sorting through junk in the attic and hauling it down where it's exposed to the clean light of day. There you can see, between the stacks of rubble, the deep injustices.

I can see Hattie Jordan. Every Thursday, when my children were little, Hattie came out on the city bus to help me. Those were the days when you had to boil baby bottles, and "real" diapers were made of cloth. I was lucky, though, because of Hattie. She worked hard. Washed and ironed—I can still hear the iron pounding the padded board, and smell the starch on stiffened shirts. Her skin was as smooth as mahogany and she had hands that could gather up a pile of laundry in one sweep, wrap the babies in terry towels, and turn a mound of dough into the miracle of buttered rolls. For seven dollars a day.

But somewhere along the way Hattie's eyes had lost the brandy-colored light that God had given them.

One day she telephoned. Her nephew had been killed in an automobile accident and she couldn't come to work. "Of course," I said, "I'm so sorry. Is there anything I can do?" There was nothing, but the egg man from the country came by the house a few days later and I bought an extra dozen eggs for her. She liked country eggs.

Hattie came back to work the next week. After I picked her up at the bus stop, she stepped out of the car and started picking up toys the children had abandoned in the driveway. When we got to the kitchen, I showed her the eggs. She looked at them and then looked at me with those dark eyes. Then she said, "Mrs. Sigloh, that boy was like a son to me, my very own. You have your son, but mine died last week, and all you did for me was buy a dozen eggs."

I never saw Hattie again. She wasn't at the bus stop the next week.

But I remember.

Over time the lens has widened, and I can see myself standing waist deep in the neglect and bigotry of our culture, but that doesn't help. Maybe it's my age, or maybe it's all the junk I've hauled down from the attic, but I'm tired of deflections and therapeutic advice about forgiving myself. I'm the Levite in the Good Samaritan story. I saw the wounded on the road to Jericho, and passed by on the other side. And blaming society, or the burden of parenthood, or the environment, or a bad hair day does nothing but block the possibility of peace. I need to do something.

But I don't know what. Restitution was spelled out so clearly in the priestly laws of Leviticus. Of course, they look a bit skewed to the modern eye, but at least they offered an intentional, concrete way of doing something: "When any of you sin and commit a trespass against the Lord by deceiving a neighbor in a matter of a deposit or a pledge, or by robbery, or if you have defrauded a neighbor, or have found something lost and lied about it. . . and realize your guilt, and would restore what you took, you shall repay the principal amount and shall add one-fifth to it. . . . And you shall bring to the priest, as your guilt offering to the Lord, a ram without blemish from the flock, or its equivalent, for a guilt offering" (Leviticus 6:1-6).

The language of the law was frankly financial, arising as it did out of a mercantile society, but using its terms as metaphors, I would gladly repay the "principal amount" of humanity I stole from Hattie Jordan and add one-fifth. Unfortunately, Hattie Jordan has crossed over to the other side, so I can't even try to do that. Restitution is no longer possible. And even if it were, the aching residue of guilt would linger.

I guess that's why the law stipulates a guilt offering. I don't have an unblemished ram to offer the Lord. In fact, I don't have a *blemished* ram to offer. And it's a fearful thing to stand in the presence of the living God—especially when we stand empty-handed. In the words of Walter Brueggemann:

> Communion with the holy one is nearly more than we can bear, because we shrink from a meeting shaped by a *massive sovereignty* before which we bow, or by *suffering love* that is self-giving. . . . The risk is too great, the discomfort so demanding. We much prefer to settle for a less demanding, less overwhelming meeting. Yet we are haunted by the awareness that only this overwhelming meeting gives life.[68]

So we slip in the back door and prepare to bow before the massive sovereignty of God. The accountant in the front office takes down our name and Social Security number. It's nearly more than we can bear, but like petitioners in a bankruptcy court, we hand over our list of debts. The celestial accountant enters them on a spread sheet. It takes forever, and the column is very, very long. We wait—wondering how we will pay, feeling the weight, heavy like stone.

Then the accountant looks up with a smile. "Madam . . . Sir . . . it seems that your bill has been paid."

"What? That can't be."

"But it is. See for yourself . . . right here on the bottom line it says, 'Account paid in full.'"

Imagine such a thing. Every debt paid, cancelled, deleted in one stroke, one death, one cross traced across the thin air. What a reckoning. It's the other side of massive sovereignty. It's the "suffering love that is self-giving." The anguish that overrides the wrath.

> I thought how I would set you among my children,
>   and give you a pleasant land,
> the most beautiful heritage of all the nations.
> And I thought you would call me My Father,
> and would not turn from following me. (Jeremiah 3:19)

But even in God's anguish, it is God's very nature to override— generously, passionately, recklessly—the aching residue of guilt that lingers.

And that's not the end of it all. In the wake of God's reckoning we long to make greater restitution, not out of *obligation* but out of *gratitude* because the debt has been cancelled. Then gratitude begets life which begets love which begets life which begets love. In an endless network of grace.

And so for awhile longer I'll walk in the front door carrying whatever pitiful offering I can. But someday, when this body is destroyed, and I stand in the presence of the living God, I'll carry a basket filled with dozens and dozens of fresh country eggs. And I'll ask to see a beautiful woman named Hattie Jordan.

30

The Great Nevertheless

I SEE people on roller blades these days and I wonder at the ease of the sport. When I was young, we had to attach skates to our shoes with a metal key. The skates were awkward and uncomfortable, but if you were a good skater, you could set up a rhythm with the clicking of wheels across cracks in the sidewalk. Then at the end of the block, you turned—toes-out and arms extended—like Sonja Heine on ice. Sister Carolyn and I were good skaters.

But Ben Barbee, who lived next door, didn't like for us to skate. He wanted us to climb trees with him and crawl onto the roof of the porch. So one day he threw gravel on the sidewalk. I tripped and had to wear a cast on my ankle the rest of the summer. I hated Ben Barbee. He didn't even say he was sorry.

Fortunately, the impact of transgressions like his diminish in magnitude as the years go by. Hate melts like an early frost. But in the rarefied atmosphere of old age we have a lot more time to dwell on the transgressions of others. And dwell we will. On the time that . . . the words that. . . . Sometimes resentment lasts for decades, especially when we nourish it. In his poem, "The Poison Tree," William Blake describes what happens when we nourish it:

And I watered it in fears,
Night and morning with my tears;
And I sunned it with smiles
And with soft deceitful wiles.[69]

In Blake's poem, injury and hidden anger combine to produce a poison that's fatal. That's why "the good book" keeps telling us to be reconciled. "So when you are offering your gift at the altar, if you remember that your brother or sister has something against you, leave your gift there before the altar and go; first be reconciled to your brother or sister, and then come and offer your gift" (Matthew 5:23-24).

Reconciliation is easy when the transgression is just gravel on the sidewalk, but when it's more serious, you have to swallow your pride and spit out the poison.

You have to pretend you're the Prodigal's mother. She was the one who had two daughters, a good one and a bad one. The older daughter had a steady job, kept her room nice and neat, and remembered to send birthday cards to all the family. But the younger one was the mean and restless sort. She didn't remember anyone. Her jobs were now and then. And her room was a disaster area.

One day the younger sister said to her mother, "Mama, can I have some of your money now, like . . . before you die, so I can be on my own? I'm tired of this place. Same thing every day. Get up. Go to work. Come home. Eat supper. Watch TV. Day after day. Same thing. I gotta get outta here."

And so the woman pondered her daughter's request. "Why would she want out of here? Home is heaven. And does she want me dead before my time? Surely not, and yet she says, "Can I have some of your money now?" It will be a heavy loss to let her go, but how can I refuse? After all, she's my child. It was I who taught her how to walk."

So the woman cashed in her life insurance, took out a second mortgage, and gave all the money, in clean new bills, to her daughter, the mean and restless one. The daughter went away—beyond the horizon—following a life of ease and luxury. She spent her mother's money on expensive clothes and sweet perfume, on summer gowns with see-through lace. She lolled around the house all day, and when the lights came on across town, she went out dancing in the disco bars.

Then it was gone. All the money was gone. And she had nothing to eat. She remembered how her mother fed the guests at her table. I will go to my mother and I will say, "Mama, I have sinned against heaven and before you. I am no longer worthy to be called your daughter. Treat me like the least of these and I will be happy." So she got on the bus and started for home.

Her mother didn't know she was coming, but she was waiting—looking out the window, just in case. And when she saw a swirl of dust rising up off the road, she rushed out the door. Didn't even wait for the bus to stop before she ran to meet it. "It's my daughter!" she cried. And when the girl stepped off the bus, the woman wrapped her arms around her and said, "It's okay." Before the girl could open her mouth and apologize, she said, "It's okay. You're home now."

And the woman called out to friends in the neighborhood. "Quickly . . . bring that new silk scarf from my closet. Put it over her shoulders. And put sandals on her feet, and my grandmother's ring on her finger, the one with sapphires circled in gold." Then she said, "Let's have a barbecue tonight, with corn on the cob and ripe tomatoes and apple pie for dessert. This child of mine was dead and now she's alive. She was lost and now she's found."

But the older sister wasn't pleased with all the hoopla. After all, she'd stayed at home to take care of her mother. She'd held her steady job and kept her room nice and neat, while her sister ran away with her mother's treasure and squandered it in riotous living. "Where's the justice of it all?" she complained.

By justice the older daughter meant the law of retribution—an eye for an eye, a tooth for a tooth. In other words, her sister should pay back every single penny she'd squandered before there could be a barbecue and apple pie.

But the older daughter didn't understand that forgiveness is "in spite of," not "because of." It's the "great nevertheless" of relationships.

And forgiveness isn't the same as forgetting. What's happened in the past is part of us. We can't break it off any more than we can break off our arms and throw them away. We are who we are, molded into being, broken, mended, broken again. And even though we run down the road to reconcile with those who've injured us, the memories are still there.

But we need to forgive—before it's too late. Forgive every single person who's squandered our treasure, forsaken our home, violated our trust. Every single person who's treated us with anger, deceit, neglect, sarcasm, condescension.

That's a lot of forgiveness. It could even be more than seventy times seven. But if we don't forgive, all the resentment that we've nursed and sunned with smiles and soft deceitful wiles will turn our love to gall. We can't let that happen. We just can't. Sisters and brothers need to put arms around each other—or at least shake hands—so they don't die with the taste of poison on their lips.

I think what I'll do is make a list of all the transgressions that have been committed against me, from gravel on the sidewalk to . . . the time that . . . the words that. . . . First I'll catalogue them according to omission and commission. Then I'll enter each transgression in the ledger book. With red ink. And codes to indicate severity—ten being the most severe. Then, one by one, I'll cross them off the books.

I might have to wait until next week to forgive the big ones. Or until Someone Else guides my hand across the page. Lately I've had to wait a lot for Someone Else, but then on a morning out of nowhere, it happens. I'll be doing something incidental like filling the bird feeder or scraping ice off the front steps, and suddenly there's a prompting—as evanescent as a moth on the wing. Like the feeling Wordsworth had when he wrote these lines "a few miles from Tintern Abbey."

> And I have felt
> A presence that disturbs me with the joy
> Of elevated thoughts; a sense sublime
> Of something far more deeply interfused.[70]

And in that moment so much is possible. We can even forgive the big ones when we feel disturbed with the joy.

Heading
Home

31

Side by Side

WE'VE traded in our charm bracelets for Medic Alert bracelets. What a dismal switch that is. Charm bracelets jingled when we walked, fell over our cuffs in a cascade of silver. "My father gave me this one for my sixteenth birthday. This one came from Venice." Medic Alerts carry no such sentiment—only an in-case-of number.

When our daughters went to summer camp, they traded their charm bracelets for knotted strips of leather. They called the bracelets "bear scares." I could appreciate the ornaments—sort of—but I didn't understand the name.

"You see," said Sally, with the long-suffering patience that children muster when talking to grown-ups, "we tie knots in the bracelets and give them to our friends. This knot is for loyalty; this one is for fun; this one is for secrets; and the fourth one—the one that ties the bracelet together—it's to scare the bears away."

Of course.

"Bear Scares" weren't like charm bracelets, but the girls never took them off, even for dress-up occasions. Indeed, by late winter I began to think that one day they would marry and be the first brides in town to walk down the aisle wearing something old, something new, something borrowed, something blue, and something to scare the bears away.

But I think I'm beginning to understand that, even though their bracelets didn't jingle or carry an in-case-of number, they were important. Not because the girls were afraid of bears, but because the exchange of that leather strip bound them to their "best friends." Tied them together as bluebirds or finches or whatever they called themselves at camp.

And I think I'm beginning to understand how important those bonds are, not only to young girls, but also to those of us who are full of years. Maybe even *especially* to those of us who are full of years. C. S. Lewis refers to friendship as one of the four types of love: "To the Ancients, Friendship seemed the happiest and most fully human of all loves; the crown of life and the school of virtue."[71]

The modern world, of course, is reluctant to describe friendship in terms of love (it might be confused with the erotic variety), so it's been banished to a lower level of sensibility. As C. S. Lewis explained: "It is something quite marginal; not a main course in life's banquet; a diversion; something that fills up the chinks of one's time."[72]

And yet for the orphaned, the widowed, the childless, and those who must wear Medic Alerts, friendship is the crown of life. I suppose it assumes that level of importance because our extended families are preoccupied with professional and parental responsibilities. As they should be. I don't begrudge the time family members spend with each other, but good friends are constant companions. They go to the movies with you. They sit next to you in church and when it's time to leave, they remind you not to forget your prayer book.

And constancy isn't the only knot of friendship. As Sally so patiently explained, there's also loyalty, fun, secrets, and even a mutual defense against all sorts of "bears." I have a few old friends who are still alive. They are the ones who shared with me the moments of despair and ecstasy, as well as the long days of routine living. They were the ones I used to call as soon as I got home from school, or as soon as the boy down the street said he "liked" me.

There are no more phone calls now, only a Christmas card with a note attached—"Miss you so! Let's get together next year"—but we're still an intimate part of each other's past. In the mystery of relatedness, we helped each other grow up.

There are other friends now, but most of them are the kind
Judith Viorst describes in *Necessary Losses*, the kind with whom,
"We maintain our public face and emotional distance. Which
means . . . that I'll talk about being overweight but not about
being depressed. Which means I'll admit being mad but not blind
with rage. And which means I might say that we're pinched this
month but never that I'm worried sick over money."[73] We would
happily include the new friends in our leather bracelet crowd, if
we could learn to trust them enough to share the hidden edges of
our being. Who knows—maybe they too could become "best
friends."

Best friends have something that goes beyond the exclusive
nature of other friendships. C. S. Lewis says that "Lovers are nor-
mally face to face, absorbed in each other; Friends, side by side,
absorbed in some common interest."[74] Their friendship evolves
out of mutual studies, games, professions, tastes. As Lewis says,
"All who share it will be our companions; but one or two or three
who share something more will be our Friends. In this kind of
love, as Emerson said, *Do you love me?* means *Do you see the
same truth?*"[75]

It's a profound question. Do you see the same truth? It opens
the way for a common vision and a common quest—one that can
be huge and noble, as in the defeat of Grendel by Beowulf and
Hrothgar, or one that can be small and tender as the friendship in
Truman Capote's *A Christmas Memory*.

In Capote's story an old woman of childish disposition and
the boy she calls "Buddy" embark every Christmas on the ambi-
tious enterprise of baking thirty-one fruitcakes, dampened with
"daisy-yellow liquor." They send the fruitcakes to "friends," some
of whom they have met only once. And, as always, they send one
to President Roosevelt. On Christmas Eve, after the cakes have
been mailed, the two wait for the restless dawn.

> "Buddy, are you awake?" It is my friend, calling from her
> room, which is next to mine; and an instant later she is sit-
> ting on my bed holding a candle. "Well, I can't sleep a hoot,"
> she declares. "My mind's jumping like a jack rabbit. Buddy,
> do you think Mrs. Roosevelt will serve our cake at dinner?"

We huddle in the bed, and she squeezes my hand I-love-you. "Seems like your hand used to be so much smaller. I guess I hate to see you grow up. When you're grown up, will we still be friends?" I say always.[76]

I'd like for friends like that to stick around until I die. We can meet and enjoy our idle talk. Then, shortly after I die, I'd like for them to follow me, so we can take up where we left off. Not that I wish them a premature death or anything, but I'm afraid it will be lonely in our Father's house—with all those "many rooms"—if my old friends aren't there.

Unfortunately, some of them don't cooperate. They die first, leaving only an echo of our laughter. Sometimes it seems like the month is just one funeral after another. And every one of them takes away a bluebird or a finch from my flock of old friends. Every one of them takes away part of my self.

In *A Christmas Memory* years after the two friends have been separated, the boy hears that his friend has died. "And when that happens, I know it. A message saying so merely confirms a piece of news some secret vein had already received, severing from me an irreplaceable part of myself, letting it loose like a kite on a broken string."[77]

When Gilgamesh loses his friend Enkidu, he swears that he will wander in the wilderness wearing the skin of a lion. David loses his friend Jonathan and sings the "Song of the Bow:"

Your glory, O Israel, lies slain
Upon your high places!
How the mighty have fallen! (2 Samuel 1:19, 25b, 26a)

Last week I went to a funeral and we sang "What a Friend We Have in Jesus." I sang it with gusto, letting the tears roll down my cheeks because another one of the mighty had fallen. But later I wondered about that image of Jesus as a "friend." It made me a little uncomfortable. He's usually way up there in mosaics and stained glass windows. But then I remembered his last breakfast on the beach—the one in John's Gospel where he cooks fish and hash brown potatoes for his friends—Peter and Thomas and Nathanael and James and John. And then he sits down and eats with them. That's pretty cozy.

Maybe the point of the gospel is to remind us to let Jesus become human. Let him eat breakfast with us. And when the fragile bonds of human friendship are irreplaceably severed, let him sit beside us, weep with us, and say what best friends always say: "Do you see the same truth?"

32

Sweet Bells Jangled

PRESIDENT Reagan, who in 1985 may have had early concerns that he could not remember things the way he used to, spoke at a dinner honoring Senator Russell Long.

An elderly couple was getting ready for bed one night, Reagan told the crowd. The wife turned to her husband and said, "I'm just so hungry for ice cream and there isn't any in the house."

"I'll get you some," her husband offered.

"You're a dear," she said. "Vanilla with chocolate sauce. Write it down—you'll forget."

"I won't forget," he said.

"With whipped cream on top."

"Vanilla with chocolate sauce and whipped cream on top," he repeated.

"And a cherry," she said.

"And a cherry on top."

"Please write it down," she said. "I know you'll forget."

"I won't forget," he insisted. "Vanilla with chocolate sauce, whipped cream, and a cherry on top."

The husband left the house and returned after a while with a paper bag. He handed the bag to his wife in bed. She opened up the bag, and pulled out a ham sandwich.

"I told you to write it down," she said. "You forgot the mustard."[78]

There's a cruel irony in the story, given President Reagan's fate, but the audience laughed with him, and white-haired elders everywhere probably experienced a momentary relief, because their lapses in memory weren't quite as serious as those in the story. They might forget the whipped cream, but they *definitely* wouldn't forget the mustard.

Unfortunately, forgetfulness seems to be a routine consequence of age. It goes with the territory. I like the way Billy Collins describes it:

> The name of the author is the first to go
> followed obediently by the title, the plot,
> the heartbreaking conclusion, the entire novel
> which suddenly becomes one you have never read,
> never even heard of,
>
> as if, one by one, the memories you used to harbor
> decided to retire to the southern hemisphere of the brain,
> to a little fishing village where there are no phones.[79]

We not only forget the entire novel, we forget where we put our car keys. We forget names, directions, tickets, lists, coats, hats, glasses, and gloves. But while the occasional loss of memory may be troublesome, it usually isn't of serious proportions. Well . . . maybe sometimes. I left water running in the laundry sink a few months ago—totally forgetting that I had intended to bleach some old towels. The water filled the sink, flowed over the counter, into the cupboards, onto the floor, down the hall, and under the bedroom rug before I discovered what I had done. It was a household disaster of considerable proportions.

And yet, it was not of considerable proportions when compared to other disasters precipitated by dementia, especially by those brought on by the most dreaded of them all—Alzheimer's.

We don't like to talk about Alzheimer's. It's as if the very mention of the word might invoke demons. David Shenk, author of the insightful book called *The Forgetting*, writes that:

> The fear of Alzheimer's is the fear of losing your identity
> while your healthy body walks on into oblivion. It is the fear

of becoming a ghost. . . . So we avoid it. We don't read the books; we don't ask the questions; we don't visit our newly diagnosed neighbor. . . . But of course we can't truly avoid it. Alzheimer's penetrates every aging adult's consciousness just as it penetrated Aristotle's and Swift's and Tolstoy's. It seizes those who've seen it up close and those who've never given it an attentive thought. It creeps into our dreams.[80]

Apparently the disease attacks the cortex of the brain forming bundles of tangled plaque that inhibit conversation between the neurons, and the older we get, the more likely we are to become victims. There is, at the present time, no cure, and the cost of nursing care can run to the tens of thousands of dollars every year.

Alzheimer's—Good Lord, deliver us.

Victims of Alzheimer's lose their history. They lose the touchstones to their imagination and those bright shining moments when the world was full of laughter. They lose places where they walked between the drifts of windswept winter. They lose faces they once held between their hands. They lose the self. And we have to watch them walk on into oblivion. We have to stand by the side of the road and, like Ophelia, weep for minds o'erthrown.

> Now see that noble and most sovereign reason,
> Like sweet bells jangled, out of tune and harsh.
> (William Shakespeare, *Hamlet*, Act 3, Scene 1, lines 165-166)

But even though the victims of the dread disease forget everything, they're never forgotten. Never. And I believe that somehow in the miracle of God's grace they can hear what Isaiah said:

> Can a woman forget her nursing child
> or show no compassion for the child of her womb?
> Even these may forget,
> yet I will not forget you,
> See, I have inscribed you on the palms of my hands;
> (Isaiah 49:15-16)

I'm hoping that our loved ones will not only see their names inscribed in the palms of God's hand:

T-r-i-j-n-i-e
   J-a-c-k
      B-i-l-l
         G-e-o-r-g-e
            B-o-b

I'm hoping they'll discover, as if by chance, a child's book of Bible stories on the table. And as their maturity unravels, I hope they open the book and find page after page of pretty pictures. Maybe someone will read aloud the story of the good shepherd who left ninety-nine sheep in order to go out and look for the one that was lost. Who walked through rain-drenched fields, over stones and spiny broom until he found it, and lifted it up, and wrapped it in his warm cloak. Then brought it all the way home where the pastures were soft and green. And the one who was lost was never lost again.

Marking Time

OLD age is an age of detachment. Detachment from careers, honors, incomes, homes, and possessions—in favor of attachments to loved ones. And when, in our old age, a loved one dies, the loss is all the more brutal, wrenching soul from soul, leaving the other to stand alone, like a sparrow on the rooftop.

Someone says, "He's gone to be with the Lord." You think (but do not say), "he was *already* with the Lord. I want him to come back. . . please . . . come back. I'll set the table. . . ."

Friends pay courtesy calls, carrying mountains of food—platters of ham, potato salad, broccoli florets. But it's hard to swallow when loved ones die. Food sticks in the throat.

"I'm sorry . . . so sorry." What else can they say?

"I see people, as they approach me, trying to make up their minds whether they'll 'say something about it' or not," wrote C. S. Lewis in his journal following the death of his wife. "I hate it if they do, and if they don't. . . . I like best the well brought-up young men, almost boys, who walk up to me as I were a dentist, turn very red, get it over, and then edge away to the bar as quickly as they decently can. Perhaps the bereaved ought to be isolated in special settlements like lepers."[81]

Weeks pass. Snow covers the skeleton trees; the mound above the grave begins to settle—as if it belonged there; a harbinger of spring appears in the forsythia; and sorrow seems to melt away.

Then, all of a sudden, you hear a familiar tune or find a pair of work gloves on the bench, and there it is again, that deep mass of pain.

But you knew . . . you always knew that, no matter how closely you walked in each other's footsteps, husband and wife would ultimately have to separate. It was just a question of who would go first. And you lost.

It's different, though, when a child is the first to go. You're not prepared for that kind of detachment. *You* were supposed to go first. You queue up according to age, the hour you were sent into the vineyard, and you receive your wages in the proper sequence. If the order is reversed, and you lose a loved one before he's reached the edge of age, it's a miscarriage of justice! An untimely frost. Even the birds stop singing.

"O my son Absalom, my son Absalom! Would I had died instead of you, O Absalom, my son, my son" (2 Samuel 18:33).

Someone says, "God has another angel in heaven." You think (but do not say), "He wasn't an angel; he was a boy, and he sat beside me."

O God, you have rejected us, broken our defenses;
You have been angry; now restore us!
You have caused the land to quake;
   you have torn it open;
Repair the cracks in it, for it is tottering. (Psalm 60:1-2)

And does God answer? No. "When you are happy, so happy that you have no sense of needing Him, so happy that you are tempted to feel His claims upon you as an interruption, if you remember yourself and turn to Him with gratitude and praise, you will be—or so it feels—welcomed with open arms," writes C. S. Lewis. "But go to Him when your need is desperate, when all other help is vain, and what do you find? A door slammed in your face, and a sound of bolting and double bolting on the inside. After that, silence. You may as well turn away."[82]

The world continues its routines as if nothing has happened. People go to work, they eat sandwiches in the park, talk on the telephone, sweep the front porches. They don't know. If they did, they would stop in midstride. Because the earth has rolled out of orbit, and nothing will ever be the same again.

Trees begin to leaf out. Jonquils unfold their heads for Easter morning. Children carry fists full of them into church and stuff them into a cross made of chicken wire. People fill the pews—suspending their disbelief for one day. You're surrounded by strangers, who "provide the company in which a Yes can first appear."[83] Sunday after Sunday, leaning on memory and hope, you've shared common prayer, common bread, pain, remorse, boredom . . . transports of delight.

You say the psalm together: "I believe that I shall see the goodness of the Lord in the land of the living" (Psalm 27:13). A door opens at the back of the church, and you sense a presence. There are no words. No visions. Just a shadow of life reflected against the stone wall.

C. S. Lewis says, "I have gradually been coming to feel that the door is no longer shut and bolted. Was it my own frantic need that slammed it in my face? The time when there is nothing at all in your soul except a cry for help may be just the time when God can't give it: you are like the drowning man who can't be helped because he clutches and grabs. Perhaps your own reiterated cries deafen you to the voice you hoped to hear."[84]

The congregation is pardoned, fed, blessed, and dismissed into the bright noon. Children hunt Easter eggs—running from tree to tree with baskets of green grass in their hands. People talk easily among themselves.

"I told Sarah to take the lilies in the narthex over to Mountainside."

"Larry and Joanne are going home tomorrow. All the way to Baltimore in one day."

You enjoy the calm of ordinary life. For a brief Sunday afternoon you can breathe again.

34

Facing the Abyss

R OSE, the matriarchal character in the movie *Moonstruck*, realizes that her husband, Cosmo, is chasing women. She's not particularly angry. She's just puzzled. Why does he do something like that? Over and over again she asks the same question, but no one can give a satisfactory answer. Then one night Johnny Camarerie says, "I don't know why he does that . . . maybe he's afraid of death."

"That's it!" she says. "That's it." When Cosmo slips into the house late that evening, Rose stops him in his tracks. "Cosmo," she says, "you're going to die. No matter what you do, you're going to die."

It's a wonderful scene, and the truth is sharp. Consciousness of death threatens our whole sense of significance. It makes relationships appear transient and everything we do or say or write seems meaningless. "That bareheaded life under the grass worries one like a wasp," wrote Emily Dickinson.[85]

In Leo Tolstoy's *The Death of Ivan Ilyitch*, Ivan Ilyitch, a member of the Court of Justice, has a well-ordered, respectable life. He takes a wife (it's the proper thing to do for a person of his social rank) and finds admirable apartments. He selects the wallpapers, hangings, and furniture himself. He is pleased, and:

Any kind of spot on the table-cloth, on the draperies, any break in the curtain-cords, irritated him. He had taken so much pains in getting things in order, than any kind of harm befalling was painful to him. But on the whole, Ivan Ilyitch's life ran on, as in his opinion, life ought to run, smoothly, pleasantly, and decently. He rose at nine o'clock, drank his coffee, read the paper, then donned his uniform, and went down to court."[86]

Then Ivan Ilyitch develops a strange taste in his mouth and an uneasiness in the left side of his abdomen. He sees the doctor. The pain is worse. "DEATH came up and stood directly before him, and gazed at him."[87] But Ivan Ilyitch thinks it is impossible—impossible for human life to end—for *his* human life to end. After all, his life is so well-ordered, proper, and admirably appointed. As Judith Viorst observes in *Necessary Losses:*

We live a life in which death is denied. This doesn't mean we deny the fact that all men and women, including ourselves, are mortal. Nor does this mean we avoid the articles, seminars, TV programs which feature the now chic subject of Dying and Death. What it means is that, despite all the talk, we go about our lives with the fact of our finitude held at emotional bay. . . . Our denial of death makes it easier to walk through our days and our nights unmindful of the abyss beneath our feet.[88]

But in truth, our denial of death makes it *more* difficult to walk with the abyss beneath our feet. We consume enormous psychological energy fending off our fear of death. We replace that anxiety with other anxieties. And, like Cosmo in *Moonstruck,* we engage in trivial pursuits trying to convince ourselves that it "just ain't so." But it is so. No matter what we do, we're going to die. So we'd better get used to the fact.

If you grew up on a farm, you got used to death pretty quickly because dying was as much a part of life as birthing. Not *our* dying, of course, but the dying of animals in and around the barn. Our son, Matt, was particularly fond of cats, and every time we went to the neighbor's dairy, he'd go with us so he could play with the kittens. (There was always a new litter at the dairy). Occasionally we'd let him bring one home. But we were always concerned about the cat meeting our old dog Lelee.

So I knew what was happening when, one summer afternoon, I heard the scream. "Mommie! Mommie! Hurry! Lelee is killing the cat." I ran, but it was too late. The calico fur was loose and limp on the ground. "Is she dead?" Matt buried it in a shoebox beneath the melon vines, digging in orange dirt with fingers that streaked the tears across his face. "Lelee and the cat had a fight," he explained to his father that night. "And Lelee won."

There was such resolute acceptance in his voice. And the next day he went on with life—looking for worms in apples and marching down rows of lima beans with a wastebasket on his head. But I wondered, a few years later, if the death of the cat had in any way prepared him for the death of his father. And did he, even at a tender age, begin to understand that one day he too would die?

In Chaim Potok's book *My Name is Asher Lev,* a father helps his young son cope with the reality of death after they find a dead bird on the sidewalk:

I drew . . . the way my father looked at a bird lying on its side against the curb near our house.

"Is it dead, Papa?" I was six and could not bring myself to look at it.

"Yes," I heard him say in a sad and distant way.

"Why did it die?"

"Everything that lives must die."

"You too Papa? And Mama?"

"Yes."

"And me?"

"Yes," he said. Then he added in Yiddish, "But may it be only after you live a long and good life, my Asher."

I could not grasp it. I forced myself to look at the bird. Everything alive would one day be as still as that bird?

"Why?" I asked.

"That's the way the Robbono Shel Olom made His world, Asher."

"Why?"

"So life would be precious, Asher. Something that is
yours forever is never precious!"[89]

I guess that's why the church is intent on reminding us that
everything that lives must die. And me? Yes. "Remember that you
are dust and to dust you shall return." That in-your-face reality is
like the cold blast of winter. It quickens the heart. We no longer
"go about our lives with the fact of our finitude held at emotional
bay." The fact often casts us into the pit of despair, but when the
despair has run its course, we become so much more mindful of
how precious life really is. We want to savor every bit of whatever
is left. Sit on the back porch, and enjoy everyday life that has been
drained of its everydayness. Grill hamburgers and eat popsicles
for dessert. Savor the icy orange, and listen to the drone of an air-
plane high above our heads. Then when it's dark, help the grandchildren catch fireflies in the palms of their hands, and breathe a
word of thanks because their lives are still full of possibility.

None of that is heroic pleasure. It's just ordinary joy, a fleet-
ing moment of grace that flashes like a comet through heaven's
night. But it is so much sweeter when you know it will not last.

35

Ants in the Pants

GOD spoke to Abraham, saying: "Take your son, your only son Isaac, whom you love, and go to the land of Moriah, and offer him there as a burnt offering" (Genesis 22:2). The divine command is shocking. How could God promise descendents more numerous than the stars and then destroy the child who was destined to fulfill the promise?

But Abraham obeys: "Here I am." And when the boy asks, "Father, the fire and the wood are here, but where is the lamb for a burnt offering?" Abraham quietly assures him, "God himself will provide the lamb for a burnt offering, my son" (Genesis 22: 7-8). It's a terribly difficult story. Every time I read it, I feel an instant aversion for the One who would require the murder of a beloved son, and every time I read it, I pray "Do not put *me* to the test." But, for all its terror and dread, the story shows what it means to trust God even when God doesn't appear trustworthy. Even when God appears to be without mercy or compassion.

I could never measure up to Abraham's trust. Of course, I've not been asked to offer my son as a burnt offering. But God *has* told me that one day everything I know and love is going to end. And I'm increasingly anxious about the question: will God provide? Especially as I approach the end of my years. Ahead of me is the great abyss. Is there really a there out there?

I'd like to respond to God's promise the way Abraham responded to God's command, but as children of the enlightenment, that's very difficult. We've been trained to suspect anything that hasn't been dissected, inspected, and tested under the microscopic eye of science. Or analyzed, sterilized, and systematized under the mighty power of reason. As Peter Gomes points out, "At the center of all that knowledge, of course, is no longer 'god' but man, who has in fact now become God. That knowledge which was forbidden Adam and Eve and got them expelled from the Garden of Eden is now ours, and we have become as gods, realizing God's first and worst nightmare."[90]

In John Updike's novel *Roger's Version,* Dale Koehler thinks he can capture God on his computer. "He is giving God . . . an opportunity to declare Himself even more clearly than He has declared Himself in the preposterous odds of Creation, the miraculous aptness of the physical constants, the impossibilities of evolution, and the consciousness that flits above the circuitry of our neurons."[91] Koehler plays a game of hide and seek with God, but frequently he encounters the computer's protest of "insufficient memory." Then, while his fingers flicker across the plastic keyboard, crashing together agglomerations of vertices and parametric curves, something strange appears. It's a hand, turned upward in invitation, with fingers pointing out of the screen. "Frozen along his veins, scarcely daring breathe lest he jar loose a pivotal electron, he taps the command to take a printout of the pattern."[92] The image ripples; seconds pass and the concentric tunnels divide. Then the hand folds in and vanishes.

Science fails to print out the pattern of God's hand. But I have to remind myself that I was a child of the Promise long before I was a child of the Enlightenment. There was light shining in the darkness long before God said, "Let Newton be." And as a child of promise I learned to search for divine truth in places beside the computer and the lens of a microscope. I learned to search in music and myth and the banner of stars in the sky.

> The heavens tell out the glory of God,
> the vault of heaven reveals his handiwork.
> One day speaks to another,
> night with night shares its knowledge,
> and this without speech or language
> or sound of any voice.

Their music goes out through all the earth,
their words reach to the ends of the world. (Psalm 19:1-4)

The search continues, but still, when the vault of heaven
reveals nothing but darkness between the stars, I wonder.

Abraham leads his son, step by measured step, up the slopes
of Mt. Moriah. There he builds an altar, places the wood in order,
binds the boy and lays him on top of the wood. Then he reaches
out his hand and takes the knife to kill his son. At that point the
drama is suspended, as I am, by the question, "Where is the
lamb?" Then "Abraham looked up and saw a ram, caught in a
thicket by its horns. Abraham went and took the ram and offered
it up as a burnt offering instead of his son. So Abraham called that
place 'The Lord will provide'" (Genesis 22:13-14).

Abraham believed and it was reckoned to him as righteousness. But how much doubt did he repress even as he believed? Did
his heart rebel in anguish at the inscrutable will of a God who
would put him to such a test? And when you get right down to it,
isn't there always a "no" behind the "yes?"

"I believe. Lord, help my unbelief."

Frederick Buechner defines doubt as "the ants in the pants of
faith. They keep it awake and moving."[93] In which case, doubt is
one of the gifts of older age, because we definitely have a lot of
ants in the pants as we approach the great abyss. Complacency—
nurtured by preachers who've scattered their blessings like con-
fetti on the street—gives way to questions. Like Thomas, we want
to dig our fingers into Christ's side. Feel the warmth and truth of
his wounds. And trust that his new life will be our new life.

I believe. Lord, help my unbelief.

I've decided we should erase the noun *faith* from our language. Nouns are static. Instead, the whole process of walking up
Mt. Moriah with Abraham's trust should be captured in a verb.
And when someone comes up to us and says, "Do you have
faith?" we should respond, "Thank you very much. I'm faithing."
Like one who is awake and moving. Faithing falters, sometimes
quickens its beat, and sometimes falls back on clichés that are
worn mute as old pennies.

And our whole concept of faithing has changed dramatically over the ages as the writer, Martin Smith points out.

> Consider how different the experience of faith was for our forebears in medieval Catholic Europe. There the opposite of faith was heresy. . . . To question, to pose an alternative construction of reality, was madness, rebellion, a saboteur punching a hole below the water-line in the church's hull. . . . Consider how different again was the experience of our nineteenth-century forebears as the sacred canopy of meaning, the canonized Christian world-view, suffered a massive crisis of plausibility under the impact of science and modernity. Then the opposite of faith was doubt.[94]

And yet today we realize that "the truest faith springs from honest doubt."[95]

And in our pluralistic world, doubt is certainly a lot healthier than certitude. In the mystery of faithing, even the cross in my pocket resists certitude. It's a sturdy cross, carved out of red cedar by a friend of mine. It's full of whittled edges, but a few years ago a knot in the wood at the center of the cross fell away leaving an empty place. I don't know what to make of the change, but I've decided that it will be good to live to the end of my age with the open question. As R. S. Thomas said in his poem "Threshold":

> ah
> what balance is needed at
> the edges of such an abyss.
> I am alone on the surface
> of a turning planet. What
> to do but, like Michelangelo's
> Adam, put my hand
> out into unknown space,
> hoping for the reciprocating touch?[96]

I reach out, knowing that the "reciprocating touch" was nailed to the cross. Faithing, faithing, faithing. One day speaks to another. Perhaps my doubt will be reckoned to me as righteousness.

Crossing
the
Jordan

36

Angel Wings

ONE year, when my children were quite young, I received an auspicious note from school. It was a few days before the Christmas pageant and the note read: "On Friday morning the girls are to arrive at 8:30 to put on their angel wings and the boys are to arrive at 8:45 to put on their garbage bags."

I discovered that the teachers could change—within minutes— a garbage bag into a costume for soldier, sailor, shepherd, prince, pilgrim, pirate. But I was very glad that I was a "girl," given the suggestion of such a huge discrepancy in the value of the sexes. And I hope that someone up in heaven has already started measuring me for angel wings.

But before they can attach them, I have to die. I've never died before, so I don't know what to expect. I do have a mental picture of a "good death, however." I'll lie in my own bed where there is a view of the meadow beyond. The pillows will be fluffed and I'll wear my nicest gown—the one with cream-colored lace around the collar. All the children will be there, and I'll give them some last-minute advice—sort of the way Melanie gave Scarlet O'Hara last minute advice in *Gone with the Wind* ("Be good to Rhett. He loves you so"). I'll remind them that the antique quilt belongs to Sally and Ethan gets his father's guitar. Then I'll lift my hand in a final blessing and expire as in a plume of smoke.

That would be a nice way to go.

But I must admit—the picture of a "good death" notwithstanding—I'm a little afraid. Not that I think death marks the end of life. I know that the end is a beginning and that after I cross over, I'll be "wrapped in light as with a garment . . . and ride on the wings of the wind" (Psalm 104:2-3). But I have to die first. And when you're my age, death isn't something theological. It's something real. I get a whiff of it now and then.

And what scares me the most is that I have to cross over alone. I wish it could be the way it was when my sister and I jumped off the big boulder into the Frio River. We would stand together— young kids trembling in anticipation—and count. One. Two. Three. Jump! Then we'd leap, hand in hand, into the cold water.

My sister won't be able to leap with me when I die. I'll have to go it alone.

The fear of that solitary transition was the message of one of Martin Luther's most famous sermons: "The summons of death comes to us all, and no one can die for another. Everyone must fight his own battle with death by himself alone. We can shout into another's ears, but everyone must himself be prepared for the time of death, for I will not be with you then, nor you with me."[97]

Of course, the hospice movement has made it possible to have friends and family around us when we are summoned to death. But we still have to leap into the cold water alone. And what if the dying isn't the way we imagine it? What if it's the way Emily Dickinson imagined it?

> I heard a Fly buzz when I died;
>   The stillness round my form
> Was like the stillness in the air
>   Between the heaves of storm.
>
> The eyes beside had wrung them dry
>   And breaths were gathering sure
> For that last onset, when the king
>   Be witnessed in his power.
>
> I willed my keepsakes, signed away
>   What portion of me I
> Could make assignable, —and then
>   There interposed a fly,

With blue, uncertain, stumbling buzz
    Between the light and me.
And then the windows failed, and then
    I could not see to see.[98]

Family and friends in the poem expect to witness a sublime experience, a grand moment in which they see awe on the face of the dying just before she expires. It will be a "good death." And then "there interposed a fly." The image has a ghastly shock effect, reminding us of the grim realities of death. And the dying is seized with fear. "I could not see to see."

And if those in the throes of a "good death" are seized with fear, think of what those in the throes of a "bad death" must feel. Think of the people who die in the streets, on the field of battle, or in the deserted house of despair. Think of those who die of hunger and neglect. Or suddenly, violently, in unspeakable pain. Think of the One who died on the cross and suffered all of the above!

Sometimes it makes you tremble, tremble, tremble.

And yet we're called to "contemplate" that "bad death." Not so we understand it (we'll never understand it), but so it'll no longer be an event that's external to us, but one that's fused, grafted, absorbed into our own flesh. When I press the edges of my wooden cross into the palm of my hand, I begin to feel what Paul felt when he said, "I carry the marks of Jesus branded on my body" (Galatians 6:17).

Contemplation takes many forms.

And for all its pain, there's comfort in contemplating the cross.

If I ascend to heaven, you are there;
if I make my bed in Sheol, you are there.
If I take the wings of the morning
And settle at the farthest limits of the sea,
Even there your hand shall lead me,
And your right hand shall hold me fast. (Psalm 139:8-10)

It's too deep, too profound for tongue-tied expression, but it's good to know that when I leap into the cold water, I can leap with confidence. Because the right hand that holds me fast will pull me out of the depths and set me, breathless and dripping, on the other side. There'll be a rock near the shore and on it there'll be a wedding garment. With white lace around the collar. The pleats will be carefully pressed and the sleeves crossed over each other as if to receive a blessing. Near the garment—on another rock—there'll be a pair of angel wings—exactly my size.

No matter how it happens, I think it will be a good death.

37

The Other Side

I'M gambling that when life is over, it's not over. But, like most of us in our later years, I wonder what happens to us "on the other side." Jacob was "gathered to his people." David "slept with his ancestors." But what about us?

St. Augustine envisions a heavenly city: "God gathers, by His grace, so numerous a people that out of them He fills the places and restores the ranks emptied by the fallen angels."[99] Dante envisions a series of concentric circles with God in the center: "And at that mid point, with out-stretched wings, I saw more than a thousand Angels making festival, each one distinct in glow and art. I saw there, smiling to their sports and to their songs, a beauty which was gladness in the eyes of all the other saints."[100]

C. S. Lewis imagines a strange mobility among the spirits. They're able to ride a bus through different realms and choose which route to take. Those who were damned can even take excursions or holidays: "They go and play tricks on the poor daft women ye call mediums. They go and try to assert their ownership of some house that once belonged to them; and then ye get what's called a Haunting. Or they go to spy on their children. Or literary ghosts hang about public libraries to see if anyone's still reading their books."[101]

Lewis actually makes the life of the damned a bit tempting. I rather like the idea of haunting places after I'm gone, even though my ghostly presence might not be well-received. My mother was convinced that my father's ghost hovered near her—which meant, of course, that he was watching when she wrecked his car. After the accident I not only had to assure the driver of the other car that my mother was not an avenging angel (I explained that she had *tried* to stop behind him, but, unfortunately, she put her foot on the accelerator instead of the brake. And she did it again and again and again), I also had to assure my mother that my father did not know about the accident. "He was out in the field at the time—checking to see if the heavenly corn was ripe," I told her.

It's comforting sometimes to know that the dead don't know. But it can also be comforting to know that they do know. Billy Collins offers this possibility in his poem "The Dead."

> The dead are always looking down on us, they say,
> while we are putting on our shoes or making a sandwich,
> they are looking down through the glass-bottom boats
>   of heaven
> as they row themselves slowly through eternity.
>
> They watch the tops of our heads moving below on earth,
> and when we lie down in a field or on a couch,
> drugged perhaps by the hum of a warm afternoon,
> they think we are looking back at them,
>
> which makes them lift their oars and fall silent
> and wait, like parents, for us to close our eyes.[102]

I'll probably be one of those who waits like a parent for those who are moving below on earth. And I'll be hoping for a reunion with them. It'll be something like a high school reunion. We'll greet each other with great excitement. "Mary Lou, you haven't changed a bit." The men will talk about the time they won the district championship, and the women will talk about their grandchildren. We'll line up for a group photograph. Maybe I'll even have that new body that Paul promised us.

There'll be lots of unfamiliar faces as well. We'll even meet some of the folks they talk about in Ecclesiastes: "Those who ruled in their kingdoms, and made a name for themselves by their valor; those who gave counsel because they were intelligent; those who spoke in prophetic oracles . . . those who composed musical tunes, or put verses in writing. . . . Some of them have left behind a name, so that others declare their praise. But of others there is no memory; they have perished as though they had never been born" (Ecclesiastes 44:3-9).

I particularly want to meet a woman who's buried in a cemetery outside of Beaufort, South Carolina. There's no name on her headstone—just the inscription *Servant Woman*. I want to find Servant Woman in the crowd and say, "Tell me your name."

Who knows what new visions of heaven will develop in the imaginations of future generations? It's all fanciful, of course, because we can never know what happens when it's over but not really over. Eternity is on the other side. C. S. Lewis was quite clear on that point:

> Ye can know nothing of the end of all things, or nothing expressible in those terms. It may be, as the Lord said to Lady Julian, that all will be well, and all will be well, and all manner of things will be well. But it's ill talking of such questions . . . if ye are trying to leap on into eternity, if ye are trying to see the final state of all things . . . then ye ask what cannot be answered to mortal ears.[103]

Jesus never tells the disciples what the Kingdom of heaven *is*. He just tells them what it's *like*. It's like a mustard seed; it's like a bit of yeast; it's like a treasure in the field, a pearl of great price, a net thrown into the sea. Maybe Jesus wanted to reveal the mystery of the Kingdom at the same time that he concealed it. So we wouldn't ever stop looking for it.

But sometimes we don't have to look for it. It just happens in one of those thin places where the intersection of time and the eternal opens up in front of our eyes.

We had a terrible drought in Virginia a few years ago. Leaves on the dogwood trees curled up like paper; the fields were scorched; animals in the barn nipped at each other's flanks. Then in the middle of August it rained. Lord, didn't it rain. Not a gully washer, but a good slow ruzzle duzzle rain that let the earth drink up every drop. I walked outside and listened to it whisper. Let it fall on my shoulders and pool at my feet. By morning the grass started turning green again. Then the rain was over.

Kate opened the door of the barn and let the calf out into the meadow. Along with the cattle dog. And the cat. And a rabbit named Coconut. All of them together, as if they had transcended the desire to control, or nip at each other's flanks, or destroy the lesser ones. They kicked up their heels in boundless, runaway gratitude, chasing circles in the wet grass. And, of course, there was a child to lead them. It made you wonder, "How awesome is this place! This is none other than the gate of heaven" (Genesis 28:17).

I suppose when I finally reach the other side, wherever that may be, I'll realize that I've been there before. That I've seen the beginning when its mystery began to unfold like ferns in the translucent dawn, and I've seen the ending when the dry bones of summer began to live again. And seeing it, I'll realize that I've known eternity.

38

New Shoes

MY great aunt's name was Lolo. Her real name was Lomie Lee Johnson, but I called her Lolo. She lived in Providence, Rhode Island, so when I moved to Connecticut, she and I became fast friends. I'd drive up I-95 every few weeks and spend the day at her nursing home.

Lolo was the rebel-in-residence there. Every morning the ladies had to gather in the living room for worship before they could eat breakfast. She hated that, wanted to get on with her oatmeal before it got cold, but she endured it with tight-lipped silence—unless, of course, they sang "Washed in the Blood of the Lamb." Then she'd let it fly with irreverent whispers. "Not me, thank you very much. I'd rather use soap."

Lolo's religion didn't fit with the nursing home's variety. She and her friends in the academic community believed that reason had an exclusive claim on the truth, so "This business about the Trinity and Jesus being the Son of God—well, those ideas are fine for some but. . . . Don't be offended, Jane," she'd say. "I think Jesus was a *good man,* a really *good* man."

And as for Easter . . . well, for Lolo it was simply a time to be happy (reasonably happy) about the coming of spring. After the dead of winter there was a new green on the trees, and the nursing home always planted yellow pansies in the window boxes. So it was appropriate to celebrate *something.* But as far as the Easter promise of the Resurrection was concerned, forget it: "When I die, just seal up the tomb and that will be that," she'd say.

Often after such conversations, I wondered why I believed it all myself. And I'd call out to the darkness of I-95, "Show me your glory, Lord." But I never saw a blinding light or a burning bush or six-winged seraphim.

Gradually, as time went by, the rebel-in-residence began to accept without comment the morning hymns, and the fact that her oatmeal was getting cold. She didn't eat it.

She sat in a paisley chair near the window of her room where she could look out at the Seekonk River. Dust collected on her glasses. I tied a bib around her neck, and fed her chicken broth. She talked about her childhood in Vicksburg, Mississippi. About the time they brought cotton up from the levee and let it dry on the sidewalks in front of her house. She jumped from bale to bale while the river flooded its banks. And about the time she raised a flag on the Fourth of July in memory of the thirty thousand who died in the Civil War. It was on a cliff, near the caves where her mother had huddled as a child during the siege. And where, on Independence Day, the army finally crossed its rifles and surrendered.

Lolo had worn a white dress that Fourth of July and a pair of new patent leather shoes. Later she danced around the front porch, tapping her shoes to the rhythm of a song. "O Susannah, now don't you cry for me. For I come from Alabama, with a banjo on my knee." Until her father yelled down the stairs. "Lomie Lee, stop all that racket. You'll wake the dead."

She told me about the time she rode on the Illinois Central Railroad to Chicago and how she could pitch a baseball like a boy.

But soon the rivers ran together in her mind and she looked beyond the window ledge to see if the Delta Queen was sailing up Narraganset Bay.

Then one day one of the nurses called and said it was time. I drove back up I-95. Lolo refused the chicken broth. Refused the water. So I waited in the awful interim. Took a walk down by Gano Street. The hill was littered with broken bottles and empty cans, weeds and brambles. Good Friday's land.

When I got back to the room, Lolo turned her head and whispered a few dry words. I leaned closer to hear. It was something about "walking around heaven." I put the pieces of the old spiritual together for her. "I got shoes. You got shoes. All God's children got shoes. When I get to heaven I'm gonna put on my shoes and walk all over God's heaven."

"That's it." She smiled. "Shoes."

It was the last time I saw Lolo. She died a few days later. We buried her in Providence. Sealed up the tomb. And that was that.

But it's a curious thing, because even today, when the trees are windless and there's a taste of spring in the air, I can hear—somewhere in the distance—the sound of new patent leather shoes tapping out a rhythmic tune. As if to celebrate—*something*.[104]

It Is Finished

THE hummingbirds are back—earlier than expected. An intrepid male hovered at my desk window this morning. I don't know how he knew where I was, but he stared at me with dark beaded eyes as if to say, "What are you doing? I flew non-stop all the way from Colombia and you haven't even prepared sweet nectar to welcome me." I raised my head to answer him and he was gone in a whirl of iridescent wings. But he returned.

It was late afternoon and by then I had filled the feeder and taken up my summer watch at a respectful distance. The little creatures are so extraordinary. And so responsive. They suspend their flight in a perfect wheel of wind, then, when they pick up signals from the periphery, they lift off instantly to perch on tendrils of new vine. I wish I could be more like a hummingbird.

Of course, they only weigh 0.2 ounces so they're naturally nimble. We're not. We carry around a lot of excess baggage and over the years we've lost mobility. Limbs are less limber. Responses are slow, deliberate, painful. In fact, these days I'm probably more like a flightless cormorant than a hummingbird.

And inertia is compounded by the need to "finish" things. Even when it's time to leave. Before I "lift off," there's always one more thing to do. One more glass to wash, one more window to close, one more call to make, one more email, one more glance in the mirror. Which probably explains why I'm usually late to church.

In the monastic tradition a bell—signaling that it's time for prayer, meals, work, study—requires an instant response. St. Benedict wanted the monk to put down his pen without even finishing the word or crossing a "t."

For the same reason, in icons, the Virgin Mary is often depicted with a ball of yarn falling from her hand. Legend has it that the priest of the temple decided that the community needed to make a veil to separate the Holy of Holies from the sanctuary—the veil that would ultimately be rent in two at the time of Jesus' death. And so the chief priest says, "Bring me all the young women from the tribe of David, and I will choose one maiden to weave the fabric of the veil." And so they bring Mary with all the other maidens to the temple and there they cast lots. Mary receives the one that is true purple. She will prepare the veil. It is a very great honor.

She begins the task, weaving it with precious wool, inserting at the border an original design of overlapping acacia leaves. But when Gabriel appears and announces that she will bear the Christ child, she lets go of the wool. The ball of yarn falls to the floor in an instant response: Let it be. The veil was unfinished.

But are we ever really finished? I haven't finished raising my children and they're raising their own now. I write, sculpting each phrase to suit the page and still I'm not finished. I may never be. The warning, "Hurry up, please. It's time,"[105] in T. S. Eliot's *Wasteland* announces that it's closing time at an English pub. It might as well be addressed to me, or to the student who, heedless of the bell, keeps on scribbling words in the exam book until the teacher pulls it out from under his pencil, dragging a line of lead from the last syllable. "But I'm not finished!"

We're never finished. Of God alone can it be said that his work was finished at the end of the sixth day. And, even then, God left the grass for us to cut. But, according to Paul Tournier, "the pain of unfulfillment is that of our human condition itself."[106] Jesus, being fully human, suffered the same unfulfillment. He responded instantly to signals from the periphery. To those who reached out in anguish for his reciprocating touch. And yet still people didn't get it. They had eyes but could not see, ears but could not hear: "Have I been with you all this time, Philip, and you still do not know me?" (John 14:9). In the end Jesus had to let it be.

But I have a lot more to do before I let it be. I want to take my granddaughters to Rome. Drag them all over the city. Show them the Raphael Rooms—Aeneas carrying his father on his back and the angel leading Peter out of prison. The Pieta, and the gold mosaics in Santa Maria Maggiore and the Pantheon. Then, when they're tired of all that stuff, I'll take them to Piazza Navona, buy them a pair of earrings, and eat a gelato.

I want to see the roses of October, free of summer's blight and winter's fear.

I want to go back to Nova Scotia and walk down the trail of cobbles, until we find a ledge that overlooks the sea. Then wade in tidal pools, search for limpets under green and copper filigree. Bathe a little longer in the sun's largesse.

I want to know that someone else will pick up the rake that I let fall in the grass, like the old man in R. S. Thomas's poem "Good":

> The old man comes out on the hill
> and looks down to recall earlier days
> in the valley. He sees the stream shine,
> the church stand, hears the litter of
> children's voices. A chill in the flesh
> tells him that death is not far off
> now: it is the shadow under the great boughs
> of life. His garden has herbs growing.
> The kestrel goes by with fresh prey
> in its claws. The wind scatters the scent
> of wild beans. The tractor operates
> on the earth's body. His grandson is there
> plowing; his young wife fetches him
> cakes and tea and a dark smile. It is well.[107]

When I feel the chill in the flesh, see the shadow under the great boughs, I hope I can say, "As for me, I am already being poured out as a libation, and the time of my departure has come. I have fought the good fight, I have finished the race, I have kept the faith" (2 Timothy 4:6-7). I hope I can lift off with a nimble spirit, catching the breath of new life on the rise, and say with gratitude for what has been and what will be, "It is finished."

ཥ Notes

1. Hermann Hesse, "On Old Age," in *My Belief: Essays on Life and Art, 1952*. Oxford Book of Aging, page 56.

2. Hermann Hesse, 56.

3. *Two Thousand Years of Prayer,* compiled by Michael Counsell (Harrisburg, PA: Morehouse Publishing, 1999), 77.

4. Dylan Thomas, "Fern Hill," in *The Norton Anthology of Modern Poetry* (New York: W. W. Norton & Co., 1973), 910.

5. T. S. Eliot, "Burnt Norton," in *Four Quartets* (New York: Harcourt, Brace, and Co., 1943), 5.

6. Walter Brueggemann, *Theology of the Old Testament* (Minneapolis, MN: Fortress Press, 1997), 317.

7. Emily Dickenson, "There's a Certain Slant of Light," in *The Collected Poems of Emily Dickinson*, with notes and introduction by Rachael Wetzsteon, consulting editorial director, George Stade (New York: Barnes and Noble Books, 2003), 252-253.

8. C. S. Lewis, *A Grief Observed* (Minneapolis, MN: Seabury Press), 30.

9. D. H. Lawrence, "Shadows," from *The Complete Poems of D. H. Lawrence* (Wordsworth Editons Limited).

10. Dante Alighieri, *The Divine Comedy of Dante Alighieri*, Trans. by Allen Mandelbaum (New York: Bantam, 1982), 3.

11. C. S. Lewis, *Prince Caspian* (New York: Collier, 1951), 151.

12. Emily Dickinson, "Tell the Truth but Tell It Slant," in *The Norton Anthology of Modern Poetry*, ed. Richard Ellmann and Robert O'Clair (New York: W. W. Norton, 1973), 41.

13. Abraham Heschel, *The Prophets, Volume II* (New York: Harper and Row, 1962), 148.

14. Lewis, 134.

15. Phil Cousineau, *The Art of Pilgrimage: The Seeker's Guide to Making Travel Sacred* (Berkeley, CA: Conari Press, 1998), 158.

16. *Daily Reading with St. John of the Cross,* ed. Sister Elizabeth Ruth (Springfield, IL: Templegate, 1985), 30.

17. Margaret Guenther, *Toward Holy Ground* (Cambridge, MA: Cowley Publications, 1995) 69.

18. Emily Dickinson, "The Last Night that She Lived," in *The Complete Poems of Emily Dickinson*, ed. Thomas H. Johnson (Boston: Little, Brown, and Co., 1960), 497.

19. Abraham Joshua Heschel, *The Sabbath: Its Meaning for Modern Man* (Boston, MA: Shambhala, 2003), 13.

20. Heschel, 15.

21. Wayne Muller, *Sabbath: Restoring the Sacred Rhythm of Rest* (New York: Bantam, 1999), 31.

22. Gordon McQuarrie, *Stories of the Old Duck Hunters and Other Drivel* (Harrisburg, PA: Stackpole Co., 1967), 107.

23. McQuarrie, 76-77.

24. McQuarrie, 59.

25. Viktor Frankl, *Man's Search for Meaning* (New York: Simon & Schuster, 1984), 110-111.

26. Frankl, 112.

27. Paul Tournier, *Learn to Grow Old* (Louisville, KY: Westminster/ John Knox Press, 1972), 11.

28. Thomas Merton, in *Through the Year with Thomas Merton: Daily Meditations from his Writing,* ed. Thomas P. McDonnell (Garden City, NY: Doubleday, 1985), 217.

29. Paul Tournier, *Learn to Grow Old* (Louisville, KY: Westminster/ John Knox Press, 1972), 130.

30. Vicktor Frankl, 112.

31. Frankl, 115.

32. J. Philip Newell, *Listening for the Heartbeat of God: A Celtic Spirituality* (New York: Paulist Press, 1997), 2.

33. Charles Dickens, *David Copperfield* (New York: Airmont Publishing, 1965), 65.

34. John Milton, "On His Blindness," in *Great Poems in the English Language*, compiled by Wallace Alvin Briggs (New York: Tudor Publishing Co., 1941), 205.

35. John Keats, "To Homer," in *Great Poems of the English Language*, 626.

36. Esther de Waal, *Seeking God: The Way of St. Benedict* (Collegeville, MN: Liturgical Press, 1984), 86.

37. Esther de Waal, 106.

38. Esther de Waal, 113.

39. Paul Tournier, *Learn to Grow Old* (Louisville, KY: Westminster/ John Knox Press, 1991), 114.

40. Donald X. Burt, *But When You Are Older: Reflections on Coming to Age* (Collegeville, MN: Liturgical Press, 1992), 33.

41. Dylan Thomas, "The Force That through the Green Fuse Drives the Flower," in *The Norton Anthology of Modern Poetry,* ed. Richard Ellman and Robert O'Clair (New York: W. W. Norton, 1973), 903.

42. R. S. Thomas, "The Absence," in *Poems of R. S. Thomas.* (Fayetteville: University of Arkansas Press, 1985), 129. Originally published in R. S. Thomas, *Frequencies* (London: MacMillan, 1978).

43. Hymn 508, "Breathe on Me, Breath of God," in *The Hymnal 1982* (New York: Church Publishing, Inc., 1985).

44. Horton Foote, *The Trip to Bountiful,* Act II (New York: Dramatists Play Service, 1982), 42.

45. Foote, 44.

46. Foote, 64.

47. Chaim Potok, *Old Men at Midnight* (New York: Ballantine Books, 1987), 74.

48. William McNamara, *Earthly Mysticism* (New York: Crossroad, 1987), 105.

49. Walter Brueggemann, *Theology of the Old Testament: Testimony, Dispute, Advocacy* (Minneapolis, MN: Fortress Press, 1997), 685.

50. Brueggemann, 688.

51. Henri J. M. Nouwen, *Reaching Out* (New York: Doubleday, 1966), 105.

52. Julia Shields.

53. The Rev. Thom Blair, *The Vintage Voice* (Church Pension Fund Newsletter), June 2003.

54. C. S. Lewis, *The Four Loves* (San Diego: Harcourt Brace Jovanovich, 1960), 57.

55. Wallace Stegner, *The Spectator Bird* (New York: Penguin, 1990), 213.

56. Wendell Berry, "To Tanya at Christmas," in *Collected Poems 1957-1982* (New York: North Point Press, 1987), 252-253.

57. Peter Gomes, *The Good Life* (San Francisco: Harper, 1952), 167.

58. Gomes, 165.

59. Gomes, 179.

60. Jenny Joseph, "Warning," *When I Am an Old Woman I Shall Wear Purple,* ed. Sandra Martz (Watsonville, CA: Papier Mache Press, 1987), 1.

61. Kahlil Gibran, *The Prophet* (New York: Alfred A. Knopf, 1926), 19.

62. Henri J. Nouwen, *Reaching Out* (New York: Doubleday, 1986), 34.

63. Thomas Merton, from "The Sign of Jonas," in *Through the Year with Thomas Merton; Daily Meditations from his Writing,* ed. Thomas P. McDonnell (Garden City, NY: Doubleday, 1985), 217.

64. Donald X. Burt, *But When You Are Older: Reflections on Coming to Age* (Collegeville, MN: Liturgical Press, 1992), 43.

65. St. Augustine, *On 83 Diverse Questions,* 71.1, translated by Donald X. Burt.

66. Harakas, 32.

67. James Thurber, "The Moth and the Star," in *The Thurber Carnival* (New York: Harper Bros., 1945), 197.

68. Walter Brueggemann, *Finally Comes the Poet: Daring Speech for Proclamation* (Minneapolis, MN: Fortress Press, 1989), 44-45.

69. William Blake, "The Poison Tree," in *Songs of Innocence and Experience* (Oxford: Oxford University Press, 1985), 50.

70. William Wordsworth, "Lines Composed a Few Miles above Tintern Abbey," in *Great Poems of the English Language* (New York: Tudor, 1941), 374.

71. C. S. Lewis, *The Four Loves* (San Diego, CA: Harcourt Brace Jovonovich, 1960), 87.

72. Lewis, 88.

73. Judith Viorst, *Necessary Losses* (New York: Simon & Schuster, 1986), 179.

74. Lewis, 91

75. Lewis, 97.

76. Truman Capote, *A Christmas Memory* (New York: Random House, 1956), 38-39.

77. Capote, 45.

78. David Shenk, *The Forgetting: Alzheimer's: Portrait of an Epidemic* (New York: Random House, 2003), 18.

79. Billy Collins, "Forgetfulness," in *Sailing Alone around the Room* (New York: Random House, 2001), 29. Originally published in Billy Collins, *Questions about Angels* (Pittsburgh: University of Pittsburgh Press, 1999).

80. Shenk, 258.

81. C. S. Lewis, *A Grief Observed* (Minneapolis, MN: Seabury Press, 1961), 12-13.

82. C. S. Lewis, 9.

83. Martin E. Marty, *A Cry of Absence: Reflections for the Winter of the Heart* (Grand Rapids, MI: William B. Eerdmans, 1977), 178.

84. Lewis, 38.

85. Emily Dickinson, quoted in Conrad Aiken, *Emily Dickinson: A Collection of Critical Essays,* ed. Richard Sewall (Englewood Cliffs, NJ: Prentice Hall, Inc., 1963), 15.

86. Leo Tolstoy, "The Death of Ivan Ilyitch," *Tolstoy's Tales of Courage and Conflict,* ed. Charles Neider (Garden City, NY: Hanover House, 1958), 383.

87. Tolstoy, 395.

88. Judith Viorst, *Necessary Losses* (New York: Alfred A. Knopf, 1972), 306-307.

89. Chaim Potok, *My Name Is Asher Lev* (New York: Alfred A. Knopf, 1972), 156

90. Peter Gomes, *The Good Book: Reading the Bible with Mind and Heart* (New York: William Morrow and Co., 1996), 314.

91. John Updike, *Roger's Version* (New York: Fawcett Crest, 1986), 258-259.

92. Updike, 268.

93. Frederick Buechner, *Wishful Thinking: A Theological ABC* (New York: Harper & Row, 1972), 20.

94. Martin Smith, *Nativities and Passions: Words for Transformation* (Cambridge, MA: Cowley Publications, 1995), 177-178.

95. Smith, 180.

96. R. S. Thomas, "Threshold," *Poems of R. S. Thomas* (Fayetteville: University of Arkansas Press, 1985), 149-150. Originally published in R. S. Thomas, *Later Poems* (London: MacMillan, 1983).

97. Martin Luther, *Luther's Works,* ed. Jaroslav Pelikan and Helmut Lehmann, vol. 51: Sermon 1 (Philadelphia: Muhlenberg, 1959), 70, cited by Gerhard Sauter, "How Do I Encounter My Own Death?" in *Theology Today,* vol. 60, No. 4, January 2004, 501.

98. Emily Dickinson, "I Heard a Fly Buzz When I Died," in *The Collected Poems of Emily Dickinson*, with notes and introduction by Rachael Wetzsteon, consulting editorial director, George Stade (New York: Barnes and Noble Books, 2003), 252-253.

99. St. Augustine, *The City of God,* Book 22, Chapter 1 (Garden City, NY: Doubleday and Co. 1958), 509.

100. Dante Aligheiri, *The Divine Comedy,* Paradiso. Canto 21 (New York: Modern Library, 1950), 593.

101. C. S. Lewis, *The Great Divorce: A Dream* (San Francisco: Harper, 1946), 68.

102. Billy Collins, "The Dead," in *Sailing Alone around the Room* (New York: Random House, 2001), 33. Originally published in Billy Collins, *Questions about Angels* (Pittsburgh: University of Pittsburgh Press, 1999).

103. Lewis, 140.

104. Jane Engleby Sigloh, "Doubting Thomasina," in *Sermons That Work* (Cincinnati, OH: Forward Movement Publications, 1991), 17-19.

105. T. S. Eliot, "The Wasteland," in *Collected Poems, 1909-1935* (New York: Harcourt Brace and Co.), 77.

106. Paul Tournier, *Learn to Grow Old* (Louisville, KY: Westminster/ John Knox Press, 1972), 173.

107. R. S. Thomas, "Good," in *Poems of R. S. Thomas* (Fayetteville: University of Arkansas Press, 1985), 107-108. Originally published in R. S. Thomas, *Laboratories of the Spirit* (London: MacMillan, 1975).

ᨠ Bibliography

Aesop. *The Fables of Aesop*. Retold by Joseph Jacobs. New York: Macmillan Co., 1967.

Affirmative Aging: A Resource for Ministry. Minneapolis, MN: Winston Press, 1985.

Alighieri, Dante. *The Divine Comedy*. The Carlyle-Okey-Wicksteed Translation. New York: Modern Library, 1950.

Benet, William Rose, and Pearson, Norman Holmes, ed. *The Oxford Anthology of American Literature, Vol. II*. New York: Oxford University Press, 1938.

Berry, Wendell. *Collected Poems 1957-1982*. New York: North Point Press, 1987.

Blake, William. *Songs of Innocence and of Experience—Showing the Two Contrary States of the Human Soul*. Oxford: Oxford University Press, 1985.

Book of Common Prayer (New York: Church Publishing Co., 1979).

Bournke, Vernon J., ed. *Saint Augustine: The City of God*. Garden City, NY: Doubleday, 1958.

Brueggemann, Walter. *Finally Comes the Poet: Daring Speech for Proclamation*. Minneapolis, MN: Fortress Press, 1989.

Brueggemann, Walter. *The Message of the Psalms*. Minneapolis, MN: Augsburg Publishing House, 1984.

Brueggemann, Walter. *Theology of the Old Testament*. Minneapolis, MN: Fortress Press, 1997.

Buechner, Frederick. *Wishful Thinking: A Theological ABC*. New York: Harper & Row, 1973.

Burt, Donald X. *But When You Are Older: Reflections on Coming to Age*. Collegeville, MN: Liturgical Press, 1992.

Capote, Truman. *A Christmas Memory*. New York: Random House, 1956.

Collins, Billy. *Sailing Alone around the Room: New and Selected Poems.* New York: Random House, 2002.

Cousineau, Phil. *The Art of Pilgrimage: The Seeker's Guide to Making Travel Sacred.* Berkeley, CA: Conari Press, 1998.

Crane, Ronald S. *A Collection of English Poems, 1660-1800.* New York: Harper & Brothers, 1932.

DeWaal, Esther. *Seeking God: The Way of St. Benedict.* Collegeville, MN: Liturgical Press, 1984.

Dickens, Charles. *David Copperfield.* New York: Airmont Publishing Co., 1965.

Eliot, T. S. *Collected Poems, 1909-1935.* New York: Harper Brace & Co., 1936.

Eliot, T. S. *Four Quartets.* New York: Harcourt, Brace & Co., 1943.

Ellman, Richard, and O'Clair, Robert, ed. *The Norton Anthology of Modern Poetry.* New York: W. W. Norton & Co., 1973.

Foote, Horton. *The Trip to Bountiful.* New York: Dramatists Play Service, 1982.

Fowler, James W. *Stages of Faith: The Psychology of Human Development and the Quest for Meaning.* San Francisco: Harper, 1978.

Frankl, Viktor E. *Man's Search for Meaning: An Introduction to Logotherapy.* New York: Simon & Schuster, 1984.

Frost, Robert. *Complete Poems of Robert Frost.* New York: Holt, Rinehart, and Winston, 1958.

Gibran, Kahlil. *The Prophet.* New York: Alfred A. Knopf, 1923.

Gomes, Peter J. *The Good Book: Reading the Bible with Mind and Heart.* New York: William Morrow and Co., 1996.

Gomes, Peter J. *The Good Life: Truths That Last in Times of Need.* San Francisco: Harper Collins, 1952.

Great Poems of the English Language: An Anthology. Compiled by Wallace Alvin Briggs. New York: Tudor Publishing Co., 1941.

Guenther, Margaret. *Toward Holy Ground: Spiritual Directions for the Second Half of Life.* Cambridge, MA: Cowley Publications, 1995.

Harakas, Stanley S. *Toward Transfigured Life.* Minneapolis, MN: Light and Life Publishing Co., 1983.

Harris, J. Gordon. *Biblical Perspectives on Aging: God and the Elderly.* Philadelphia: Fortress Press, 1987.

Hawkins, Peter S. *The Language of Grace: Flannery O'Connor, Walker Percy, and Iris Murdoch.* Cambridge, MA: Cowley Publications, 1983.

Heschel, Abraham. *The Prophets, Volume II.* New York: Harper Torchbooks, 1955.

Heschel, Abraham Joshua. *The Sabbath: Its Meaning for Modern Man.* Boston, MA: Shambhala, 2003.

Jung, C. G. *The Archetypes and the Collective Unconscious.* Princeton, NJ: Princeton University Press, 1990.

Kafka, Franz. *The Penguin Complete Short Stories of Franz Kafka.* New York: Penguin Books, 1983.

Keating, Thomas. *Intimacy with God.* New York: Crossroad Publishing, 1996.

Kittredge, George Lyman, ed. *The Complete Works of Shakespeare.* Boston: Ginn & Co., 1936.

Lewis, C. S. *The Four Loves.* San Diego, CA: Harcourt Brace Jovanovich, 1960.

Lewis, C. S. *The Great Divorce: A Dream.* San Francisco: Harper, 1946.

Lewis, C. S. *A Grief Observed.* Minneapolis, MN: Seabury Press, 1961.

Lewis, C. S. *Prince Caspian: The Return to Narnia.* New York: Collier Books, 1970.

Luke, Helen M. *Old Age: Journey into Simplicity.* New York: Parabola Books, 1987.

MacQuarrie, Gordon. *Stories of the Old Duck Hunters and Other Drivel.* Zack Taylor ed., Harrisburg, PA: The Stackpole Co., 1967.

Marty, Martin E. *A Cry of Absence: Reflections for the Winter of the Heart.* Grand Rapids, MI: William B. Eerdmans Publishing Co., 1997.

Martz, Sandra, ed. *When I Am an Old Woman I Shall Wear Purple.* Watsonville, CA: Papier-Mache Press, 1991.

McDonnell, Thomas P., ed. *Through the Year with Thomas Merton.* Garden City, NY: Doubleday & Co., 1985.

McNamara, William. *Earthly Mysticism: Contemplation and the Life of Passionate Presence.* New York: Crossroads, 1987.

Moody, Harry R. *The Five Stages of the Soul.* New York: Anchor Books, 1997.

Muller, Wayne. *Sabbath: Restoring the Sacred Rhythm of Rest.* New York: Bantam Books, 1999.

Newell, J. Philip. *Listening for the Heartbeat of God: A Celtic Spirituality.* New York: Paulist Press, 1997.

Newell, J. Philip. *One Foot in Eden: A Celtic View of the Stages of Life.* New York: Paulist Press, 1999.

Nouwen, Henri J. M. *Reaching Out: The Three Movements of the Spiritual Life.* New York: Doubleday, 1985.

Nouwen, Henri J. M. and Gaffney, Walter J. *Aging: The Fulfillment of Life.* New York: Doubleday, 1974.

Potok, Chaim. *Old Men at Midnight.* New York: Ballantine Books, 2001.

Prayer Book and Hymnal According to the Use of the Episcopal Church. New York: Church Publishing Inc., 1982.

Rinpoche, Sogyal. *The Tibetan Book of Living and Dying.* ed. Patrick Gaffney and Andrew Harvey. San Francisco: Harper, 1994.

Ruth, Sister Elizabeth, ed. *Daily Readings with St. John of the Cross.* Springfield, IL: Templegate Publishers, 1985.

Saussy, Carroll. *The Art of Growing Old.* Minneapolis, MN: Augsburg, 1998.

Sermons That Work: Ten Prize-Winning Episcopal Sermons and Cultural Problems in Preaching to Americans. Cincinnati, OH: Forward Movement Publications, 1991.

Shenk, David. *The Forgetting: Alzheimer's: Portrait of an Epidemic.* New York: Anchor Books, 2003.

Simmons, Henry C., and Wilson, Jane. *Soulful Aging: Ministry through the Stages of Adulthood.* Macon, GA: Smyth & Helwys Publishing, 2001.

Smith, Martin L. *Nativities and Passions: Words for Transformation.* Cambridge, MA: Cowley Publications, 1995.

Stegner, Wallace. *The Spectator Bird.* New York: Penguin Books, 1990.

Steindl-Rast, David. *Gratefulness, The Heart of Prayer: An Approach to Life in Fullness.* New York: Paulist, 1984.

Steindl-Rast, David. *A Listening Heart: The Art of Contemplative Living.* New York: Crossroad, 1996.

Theology Today, Vol. 60, No. 4, January 2004. Princeton, NJ: Princeton Theological Seminary.

Thomas, R. S. *Poems of R. S. Thomas.* Fayetteville: University of Arkansas Press, 1985.

Thurber, James. *The Thurber Carnival.* New York: Harper Brothers, 1945.

Tolstoy, Count Leo N. *Tolstoy's Tales of Courage and Conflict.* Garden City, NY: Hanover House, 1958.

Tournier, Paul. *Learn to Grow Old.* Louisville, KY: Westminster/John Knox Press, 1991.

Viorst, Judith. Necessary Losses. New York: Simon & Schuster, 1986.

Williams, Rowan. *A Ray of Darkness: Sermons and Reflections.* Cambridge, MA: Cowley Publications, 1995.

Williams, William Carlos. *Selected Poems.* New York: New Directions, 1969.